ANSWERING A DONOR'S
TOUGHEST QUESTION:

So What?

SHOW YOUR IMPACT
TO RAISE MORE MONEY

GILLES GRAVELLE

So What?
Answering a Donor's Toughest Question

Copyright © 2017 Gilles Gravelle
All rights reserved

No part of this book may be reproduced, stored in a retrieval system or transmitted in any form or by any means – electronic, mechanical, photocopy, recording or otherwise without prior written permission from the author, except brief quotations in connection with reviews.

Published by Moving Missions, Lake Forest, CA. 92630
Movingmissions@gmail.com
Movingmissions.org

Moving Missions is a registered 501(c)3 nonprofit organization dedicated to helping nonprofit causes, donors, and funders achieve greater impact together.

Cover design by Anne Marie Bailey

Gravelle, Gilles.
So What? Answering a Donor's Toughest Question / Gilles Gravelle

1. Non-profit causes. 2. Fundraising. 3. Christian mission-church-parachurch. 4. Social sector.

Includes bibliographic references and index.

ISBN-13: 978-1975720506 Gravelle, Gilles.
ISBN-10: 1975720504
U.S. Retail Price: $11.95

Other Titles by the Author

Missiographics 2.0. Visualizing the Great Commission. 2015. Colorado Springs: GMI Books. [2017] Atlanta: MissioNexes.org.

The Age of Global Giving. A Practical Guide for Donors and Funding Recipients of Our Time. 2014. Pasadena: William Cary Library Publishers.

Contents

List of Figures vii

Preface ix

1. Introduction: Live Safe's Dangerous Assumption.... 1
2. Impact Isn't Just a Big Number 9
3. Impact Stories = Your Narrative 21
4. What Qualitative Evaluation Is (and Isn't) 29
5. Planning for Qualitative Impact Evaluation 41
6. On Marketing: How to Message Your Brilliance.... 67
7. Staying Up to Date 81
8. So What, Church? 87
9. Final Word: Live Safe Gets Another Chance 101

Addendum: An Impact Planning Checklist............... 105

References and Endnotes 111

Illustrations, Charts, and Tables

Illustration 1. Standard Change Model......................31
Illustration 2. Impact-Oriented Change Planning........32

Chart 1. Predictive Assumptions.....................................38
Chart 2. Dialogue Process..50

Table 1. Examples of Illustration1 Terms..................31
Table 2. Impact Insights 37
Table 3. Reverse Logic Change Model 42
Table 4. Baseline Examples 44
Table 5. Frequency of Change 54
Table 6. Case Study Strengths and Weaknesses 57
Table 7. Participatory Narrative Inquire Process 58
Table 8. Most Significant Change Process................62
Table 9. Evaluation Model Comparison 63
Table 10. Donor Experience and Journey 73
Table 11. Innovative Shifts 75
Table 12. Examples of Church Impact Goals............95

Preface

This book is a non-technical introduction to qualitative impact evaluation for nonprofit organizations, such as social sector services, faith-based ministries, mission agencies, and churches.

I hope to accomplish at least two things with this book. First, it will be immediately apparent to readers that I strongly encourage nonprofits organizations, even those with small budgets, to take impact evaluation seriously. The days of consumer marketing of feel-good causes are quickly fading. Nonprofits of all sorts owe it to their donors and funders to provide more meaningful information on the impact their causes produce. This goes beyond one-off stories and terse anecdotes that may not accurately reflect reality.

Secondly, if your organization doesn't do impact evaluation on a regular basis, then you really don't know how much positive change you are producing. You may have a guess, but until you look more closely it remains unclear. This is a problem, because these days more donors are tired of the quantification of impact producing unverified grandiose claims of success in numbers. Instead, they want to hear about the transformational change behind the numbers.

There is a lot of literature on qualitative impact evaluation, most of which is academically dense and long. In this book I've attempted to make the topic more accessible to nonprofit leaders and their volunteer staff who don't have the time or budget to become subject matter experts. You just need some basic practical information to get started.

As the book subtitle suggests, you may be surprised how your new and improved impact reports for donors really do release more giving. The key word here is *release*. A lot of people could give more yet they don't. They are afraid it will be wasted on causes that don't produce much impact. They are motivated to release more resources when they see how successful an organization is. But you can't show how worthy your organization is unless you have good impact data to share with them.

This book should help launch you on the road to gathering clear, compelling, and reliable impact data.

A Word About Terminology

There are several terms used in the nonprofit industry to refer to people who provide money for causes. In this book the term donor will generally refer to people who support nonprofit causes through monetary gifts, donations, or grants.

Some financial contributors don't like the term donor. Giver is also used to describe them. Giver has a biblical foundation, so for faith-based supporters the term seems apt. Donor and giver will be used interchangeably.

Funder is a term generally used to describe funding organizations, such as giving groups, foundations, or other kinds of grant-making organizations. Some of these organizations prefer resource partner or financial investor. I'll use funder to cover both of these terms.

Two terms that seem to be used interchangeably in literature are high net worth and high capacity donor. It simply means they have a capacity to give much more than the average donor, hence the phrase high capacity donor. Although fewer in number, this group accounts for 72% of all giving, around $250 billion dollars annually. I use these two terms broadly to describe people who are capable of making annual donations of at five figures or more.

1.

Introduction

Definition: So what

A reply to an unimportant or irrelevant statement, indicating indifference on the part of the speaker.[1]

Live Safe's Dangerous Assumption

Live Safe's chief fundraiser was full of confidence facing the Foundation proposal reviewer. It had taken him a year of relationship building to get an appointment with this influential funder. He went into the meeting armed with reams of statistical data, ready to prove Live Safe's effectiveness. Proof of impact was in the numbers.

During the previous year Live Safe had dug, drilled, or piped water into 153 poor rural villages. The total number of people impacted by the the project was 13,158. The amount of sanitary water provided for each village was 425 gallons per day. That's a daily average of five gallons of clean water per person. His organization had provided 23,734,125 gallons of pure liquid health that year.

The fundraiser's presentation graphics were impressive and the photos stunning. Lush green fields and azure blue skies provided a backdrop to the children's smiling faces. The anecdotal stories from some of the project beneficiaries were heartwarming. Finishing the presentation, he sat down feeling confident he had established his organization as a worthy funding recipient.

This particular foundation cared a lot about children's health and welfare. It was their central funding focus, so the questions began. The reviewer started with one simple question, "So what?" Before the fundraiser could respond, she continued with another question. "Now that children are drinking sanitary water; what difference is that making in their day-to-day lives?" She went on, "How has access to clean water impacted the parents and the rest of the family? What do they understand about clean water? Have any unintended negative consequences occurred because of the water projects? Are there any happy surprises? How does having clean water contribute to their economic development?"

The fundraiser was stunned. He had no answers to her questions, so he muttered something about how difficult it is to evaluate attitudes concerning water projects. "Besides," he countered, "that sort of information would need to be scientifically-validated. The important thing is, our statistical results show children's health will improve if they keep drinking the clean water, so all will be good."

The project reviewer wasn't convinced by his statistical data argument. She needed more. He left the meeting without a funding commitment. Getting a second chance with the busy foundation leader was highly unlikely.

What Went Wrong?

Simply stated, the Live Safe presenter didn't pass the so-what test. Live Safe was operating on the simple yet dangerous assumption that just producing outcomes—people drinking sanitary water—is enough to generate lasting impact on an increasing scale. And they thought the donor would agree. Their simple theory of change was based on the conventional logic that all you need to do is produce things. The things will be adopted and continue to spread.

A major miscalculation was not carefully researching the family foundation to find out what matters most to them in the projects they fund. The fundraiser assumed they would be impressed with their statistical proof because it represents scale. People love scale. A lot of people now have sanitary water!

The foundation reviewer was not impressed by numerical impact alone. She knew the foundation only invests in initiatives that demonstrate quality change leading to improved lives. They needed more than numbers. They needed qualitative evidence showing how improved health from sanitary water was making other areas of a child's life better. What about things, such as fewer lost school days due to improved health and hygiene? Parents learn how water becomes contaminated and how to avoid that. Money spent on food instead of medicine. These is social proof of success.

The experienced proposal reviewer knew another thing the fundraiser wasn't prepared to discuss. Things don't always go wonderfully according to plan, especially with development work among the poor. What sorts of challenges and setbacks had to be overcome? This is also helpful information for a potential donor.

How did free sanitary water along with the infrastructure to deliver it impact the community at large? Were the beneficiaries involved in project planning from the start? Were local job skills developed around the project? Was the project done in partnership with local health agencies? These are things that contribute to *sustainable* development.

Serious funders want to know how positive change is a result of your methods and not just a one-time effect. More people will adopt the ideas, thus increasing social and spiritual benefit. It's not just about quantity. It's also about quality.

Most organizations define themselves by their activities; all the things they do. Instead, they need to define themselves by the transformational impact they produce. This is what donors prefer to hear about these days because it demonstrates value.

Outcomes expressed by numbers are only impressive when we know the lasting quality those numbers represent. Doing impact evaluation makes the numbers reporting far more significant.

Impact Evaluation is Not That Hard

Jason Saul, author of *The End of Fundraising*, says most nonprofits don't measure impact because they don't think it's possible. They think it's not possible because they haven't tried. He says outcomes—what I'm calling impact—is the real currency of the new donor market place.[2]

Gathering qualitative impact information is not as hard as you think. Results don't necessarily have to be scientifically proven. Your evaluation process doesn't even need to be based on any particular "accepted" theory. It only requires some small, rich samplings from various individuals and groups to discover what is really happening as a result of your work. The data you gather doesn't need to be exhaustive. It simply needs to provide some significant windows of insight into the project beneficiaries' life; hearing their stories, testimonies and complaints.

This sort of information requires interpretation. Project evaluators need to determine what it means to their organization. It is progressive learning. It may require a follow-up visit to seek answers to new questions that arose from previous interviews. It is participatory, ensuring project beneficiaries' voices help shape the study to provide the data.

Everyone benefits from this sort of learning. The organization has a better idea about how effective their methods are. The project workers know how successful their work is. The people served by the project feel ownership because they help evaluate the results and improve it. Donors have greater confidence in giving because they have a clearer understanding of project successes, failures, and lasting effects.

This book will help you understand several things:

1. Arguments to Convince the Boss

If you are not in the position to make leadership decisions for your organization, then you need to be able to convince leadership about the importance of doing qualitative evaluation. This book will provide you with some arguments to help you accomplish that.

It is not just about fundraising. Organizations that do qualitative impact evaluation are learning organizations. They discover areas of strengths and weaknesses. Learning improves processes which lead to greater impact. This releases donor giving. Indeed, the reality of funding needs drives you to demonstrate effectiveness so funders will want to participate in your mission.

2. Understanding Qualitative Evaluation

Apart from the academic-sounding phrase "qualitative evaluation," doing it is not necessarily an academic exercise. Sure, there are lots of books that can guide you through an academic discussion on the topic, but that is not the purpose of this book. You just want to gain a window of understanding into the lives of the people your organization serves. You want to confirm positive change is directly or indirectly correlated with your methods. It proves your process works and it is reproducible. Then you know the kind of impact you are making and will continue to make.

3. Ways to Do Qualitative Impact Evaluation

The good news is, because this kind of evaluation is not based on any one theory nor does it privilege one theory over another, you don't have to worry about impressing theoretically-bent pros, as if that was possible.

Practically speaking, there are many ways to look for quality change stemming from your work. Methods should fit your unique situation, seeking the kind of information that is most important to you. This book will provide evaluation options that can serve you best.

Be assured that qualitative evaluation is hard to mess up given the diversity of methods you can draw from. The removal of pressure to produce scientific results should make you feel more at ease. Still, carelessness can tarnish the data at best or ruin the evaluation effort at worst. Striking a balance is key because doing too little may not provide the data you need to convince high capacity donors. Going too far down the wrong path can be expensive and time wasting which could leave a bad taste for doing further evaluation. Hopefully, this brief book will help you strike that important balance.

4. Planning an Evaluation

When it comes to doing any sort of impact evaluation, people are either reticent or eager. When starting out, both types tend to jump into the process before asking themselves some important questions. The answers may affect other areas of your organization.

For example, how much do you budget for evaluation? CFO's see costs, donors see overhead, neither tend to see how evaluation is central to your success. Success attracts serious donors. We'll discuss some of those questions.

5. Messaging Your Evaluation Data

How you report the data depends on who you are talking to, such as internal partners, external partners, donors, funders, government agencies, and civic organizations. Be honest about your methods. It is not necessarily scientific. Rather, it is observational interpretive close approximations. That's usually enough for most donors. We'll discuss how to communicate impact in uncomplicated compelling ways.

Speaking of messaging, you may be living on borrowed time in your understanding of how you should talk about impact. More people are doing their own research than ever before. Researching an organization is most popular among Millennials, but Gen X and Baby Boomers are taking a closer look at things too. Will your message resonate with these emerging donors, or will it turn them off? We'll talk about your narrative and how to build one that reaches a wider crowd more relevantly these days.

Finally, we will also cover the importance of outside or third-party evaluations, along with consultant guidance in planning an evaluation. Third-party observers and outside consultants ask significant questions you might not have considered. Because they are not part of your organization, their questions may seem uninformed or naïve. Even so, their questions are often pretty helpful for working teams who tend to develop group think over time.

2.

Impact Isn't Just a Big Number

Once upon a time, donors were impressed by large statistical results. If making a gift to a charity helped a lot of people, then the generous giver was happy. Seeing how the givers were happy, nonprofit organizations found more ways to provide statistical results of their work. The bigger the number, the more impressive the impact. It has literally been that simple. Even these days in the social and faith sector, when people use the word "impact" it usually refers to quantity.

Of course more astute donors weren't satisfied with a simple bottom-line number. They wanted to know the statistical evaluation was done with scientific precision. Quantitative measurement had to apply an appropriate algorithm. Error rates had to be calculated along with mathematical variations. Knowing that an expert was actually trying to determine statistical impact with accuracy provided a level of assurance to these donors.

Performance measurement typically utilized numerical reports, such as jobs created, people trained, vaccines given, churches planted and people baptized. After all, people were performing a necessary activity to produce an outcome. Performance evaluation confirmed outcomes that could be counted, so donor reports typically looked like this:

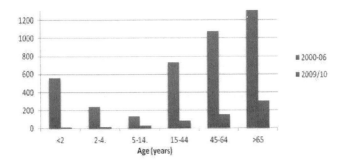

Even so, the practice of reporting numbers as impact to impress donors is losing persuasive power these days. For one reason, reports don't typically provide explanations about how an organization came up with their impact number. When a mission agency tells their supporters that during the year 1,250 new churches were started in a non-Christian country, the supporters have to take the report on trust. The problem is, supporter trust in numbers is weakening.

Because of the long-standing practice of providing large numbers without validation, donors are increasingly skeptical over grandiose numerical claims of success. If this becomes a repeated practice, the donors begin to doubt the claims are true. Stories begin to circulate about double counting. This is when different agencies claim the same results. It's not easy to validate really large numbers. So for the sake of fundraising, some agency leaders may choose to overestimate rather than understate results.

To boost credibility with donors, agency leaders need to provide explanations about how they arrived at their impact figure. Describe the methods you used to gather the information. Explain what you did to verify it. Admit when you have doubts about some of your sources or numbers.

Ultimately, you should develop a standard practice for verifying your numerical data as best you can before using those numbers in donor reports and fundraising campaigns. The more validation you can provide; the more believable your big success numbers will be.

Unfortunately, many nonprofits, especially faith-based organizations, do not provide this kind of supporting information. A simple tally is all they care about. The bigger the number, the more impressive the results. It's not a small problem.

Addressing success in numbers, Christopher Wright of Langham Partnership International said, "We cannot build the kingdom of the God of truth on foundations of dishonesty. Yet in our craving for 'success' and 'results' we are tempted to sacrifice our integrity with distorted or exaggerated claims that amount to lies."[3]

We can assume most agencies don't intentionally lie about their numerical results. However, not explaining how they verify their data in credible ways makes them look less credible to observers, especially potential donors.

Don't fail the credibility test with unverified numbers. Here are some ways to bolster the believability of your reports.

- Self-Reporting

    The best people to help confirm the numbers are the ones being counted. Use a method that helps the effected people self-report the impact, like a new church in their village. Develop a method to collect self-reported data. Combining these reports with other indicators help confirm the number you want to share with donors.

- Partnership Reporting

    These days, few organizations work independently. Usually there are a few like-minded agencies collaborating to address a need. Each organization may have a different perspective on the success of your combined efforts. Send your data report to them and ask for their feedback. Ask them how they could help improve and confirm the data.

- Third-Party Observations

    Ask a neutral third party observer familiar with the project to comment on your report. You could take it a step further and employ a third party to review your results up close.

Even if you are good at verifying numbers, there is still the other so-what test looming before you. What difference is 1,250 new churches making in people and their community? This is the qualitative information that can truly confirm the value of your organization. Knowing the *stories* behind your large impact number will make the number more impressive.

Evaluation experts often say outcomes are the results of something provided, but is that accurate? Is success the provision of a service or product? Change begins to happen now that something has been provided, yet few nonprofits spend time monitoring the process of change after their services have been rendered.

Having large numbers of things produced and in place could be significant or it could mean large numbers of things are going unused. The things you produce exist for a good reason, but is the reason being achieved? Are people being changed because of it? Thinking about impact beyond numbers is critical to your organization's success.

Think of qualitative impact as the intangible things that are difficult to count. It doesn't mean you won't try to count them later. Applying a mixed method approach of quantitative and qualitative impact evaluation will be covered later in this book.

Impact Isn't Just a Cliché Either

Both social sector and faith-based development agencies need to think beyond numbers by also talking about change. Most would argue they do talk about change. But how you talk about change is also changing. Professor and nonprofit development blogger Bruce Wydick bluntly warned, "There is a waning tolerance for clichés, positive anecdotes, and feel-good marketing in favor of solid evidence of impact." He says faith-based—and I would add social sector—development organizations need to establish impact measurement on program beneficiaries that are honest and transparent.[4]

Wydick isn't the only critic of one-off stories that don't paint a complete picture. Nigerian novelist Chimamanda Ngozi Adichie said, "Show a people as one thing, and only one thing over and over again, and that is what they become."[5] Her point is, people's stories can't be captured in only one story. There are many overlapping stories. So often impact stories focus on one single story, ignoring the other stories that define the person or the community. Not all of their stories are about tragedy, yet it's the tragic stories that generate donations. So the person portrayed, like an orphan, becomes only that to the fundraising audience.

Ken Stern, author of *With Charity for All*, says a quest for donor dollars "push charities toward happy anecdotes and inspiring narrative than toward careful planning, research, and evidence-based investments."[6]

Clichés and one-off stories are not necessarily bad. Where would nonprofit websites be without them! To build support among donors, nonprofit charities need to invest more in knowing the extent of their impact on project beneficiaries. It means telling the complete story of failures, learning, improving, in addition to the good things. That sort of transparency builds more trust between an organization and their funding partners. In other words, following that course should release more donor giving.

After doing a webinar on fundraising and impact evaluation, one participant expressed doubt that donors want this sort of qualitative information. His experience was the opposite. They were asking him for the numbers. My response was to give his donors more than they expect. Surprise them by giving them numbers with stories about quality change in the project beneficiaries' life. Then see how his donor's react to that kind of information.

My educated guess is that they will be delighted because many donors don't think it's possible to measure quality change, so they don't ask for it. They hope an anecdote or one-off story represents broad results.

Impact is About Quality Change

The trend in giving primarily for impact isn't just a story. Research shows how high net worth givers have changed their primary reason for giving over the last seven years.

- A 2007 Bank of America study of high net worth households revealed that making an impact was the 12th out of 16 reasons for giving. Maybe the donors surveyed had low expectations because only 20 percent of them believed their donations made a major impact on the causes they support.[7]

- A 2010 high net worth philanthropy report noted the most important decision for giving was based on personal experience or knowledge of the organization. Donors also depended on the opinion of families and friends. An organization's communication about impact was next, even ahead of third party ratings. Winds of change were blowing in the house of philanthropy.[8]

- In 2011, the author of *Leap of Reason* uttered these prophetic words, "Private funders will migrate away from organizations with stirring stories alone, toward well-managed

- organizations that can also demonstrate meaningful, lasting impact."9

- By 2013 more experts were talking about impact. Take for example Ken Stern's comment, "What makes these charities worthy of note is not necessarily the lightning bolt of inspiration but the rigor taken in building the organization and the care in assessing the impact of its services…"

- As of 2014, the Philanthropic Landscape report stated the number one reason for major gift giving was the impact a gift can make.10

- Now in 2017, one philanthropy expert is calling for funders to provide $500 million, collectively, for researching impact. He put it this way: "What's ridiculous is for America to give away [more than] $300 billion a year and not have any idea what impact it's having." He called it decadence.11

You may not be hearing this from your donors, but according to surveys this is apparently what they are thinking. How will you respond?

High capacity donors tend to move in circles with other high capacity donors. They hear about one another's giving experiences. Bad experiences reach the ears of others in their giving networks, and that does not bode well for the nonprofit agency that produced the bad experience. On the other hand, good giving stories are like an ocean breeze to busy people who want to make a difference with their giving. A refreshing word now emerging in these giving circles is "impact."

Over dinner at a major donor fundraising event, I struck up a conversation with a woman seated next to me. I learned it was the second time she was attending the annual event, so I asked what brought her back. "It's because of impact," she frankly responded.

I asked her to explain. She said, "With this organization, I know the kind of impact my giving is having on people. I didn't know about impact with other organizations I have supported. Now I've brought some friends to this event so they can enjoy the same giving experience I'm having." Later that evening, I was surprised to see her husband standing on stage making a funding appeal to his peers for the charity.

Hearing the stories of how project beneficiaries were changing for the better brought them into a deeper relationship with the organization and their cause. It's like a high-performing stock market investment. Now they were investing their time, as well as their money, to produce even more impact with this organization. And they were bringing their giving friends in on it!

People like this woman and her husband don't want to just reach a group. They don't want to just raise awareness about problems. They want to help solve social and spiritual problems which produces quality change in people's lives. Therefore, donor reports should explain in clear measurable terms how people are better off because of their work.

Donor Anxiety Relief

Most organizations market to donors in one of two ways. They either use broad emotional appeals to generate a gift or they go out of their way to demonstrate how trustworthy their organization is. Some organizations do both. We've already discussed the former, so let's consider the latter.

Jason Saul says nonprofits market to reduce anxiety rather than produce excitement and confidence.[12] Therefore, they talk about how well their organization is run, how low their overhead is, and the percentage of giving dollars directly benefiting their cause. As Saul puts

2. IMPACT ISN'T JUST A BIG NUMBER 17

it, "People are looking for comfort that their money will not be wasted," so this sort of information is said to be "comforting."

Givers are indeed more worried these days about wasting money on causes that are ineffective at best or using much of their money for high salaries at worst. Because of this, there are now several organizations—mostly web-based services—that help reduce donor anxiety. They do this by providing due diligence mostly through research, and then they recommend which charities to give to. For example:

- *GiveWell.org* does independent literature reviews, examines tax records, interviews organization officers, and reviews strengths and weaknesses.

- *ROIministry.org* focuses on the qualification element and the quantification element. Serving the faith sector, their due diligence adds spiritual components to their research. They determine if a ministry qualifies as a sound organization based on certain spiritual criteria, such as being Christ-centered. The quantification element confirms how much of a good thing an agency is producing in numerical terms. They will also provide third-party results analysis for a cost.

- *ExcellenceInGiving.com* provides a wide variety of services to help people be informed givers. They do extensive analytical evaluations of nonprofit organizations to help you choose the best ones. Their personalized services help donors discover their giving passion. They even evaluate results of the organizations you have supported. It's due diligence par excellence, if you have the budget for this service level.

These kinds of organizations are like an *Angie's List* for donation making.[13] They work to take the anxiety or fear out of giving because people simply don't have time to do in-depth research. Even those who do have time often don't know where to start.

These services can help donors feel more relaxed about their giving, knowing it's probably not being wasted. They may even be encouraged knowing something about the difference they are making. But is all of this really enough to engage donors for the long term, to motivate them to release even more giving, or to advocate for your organization?

In a way, it seems somewhat misguided because these services miss the most important metric of all, the lasting qualitative impact an organization makes on people.

There may be a few reasons for this. First, like most people, the due diligence websites probably assume qualitative impact can't be measured, at least through literature and website reviews. Even even if they wanted to provide due diligence in the area of qualitative impact, they would need to understand what a charity's impact goals are. The problem is, most charities lack clarity on what their qualitative impact is.

As Stern points out, charity rankings are mostly based on programmatic spending, on outputs and other countable things. But those things say nothing about organizational effectiveness in the area of impact. Not addressing impact ignores perhaps the most important criterion for giving. At least, it should be seen as one of the most important. Yet who is educating donors in this area? Not these due diligence service websites.

There are few, if any, websites that educate donors on looking for the impact an organization produces with their money. That may be impossible if organizations are not prepared to demonstrate impact in their marketing materials.

Another area of anxiety Stern points out is donors not knowing if they are helping or hurting the people the organization serves. By that I mean, are the organization's methods helping the people they serve to raise themselves out of their situations? Do the people develop improved self-worth and self-esteem? Are they developing a self-sustainable existence? Or are the beneficiaries' problems only being addressed in superficial short-term ways? These are some of the quality questions few nonprofits address. Still, donors should feel some anxiety if they can't be sure they aren't hurting rather than helping people through their giving. To relieve this kind of anxiety, nonprofits need to produce qualitative reports on these less tangible areas. The trouble is, many organizations really don't know the effects of their methods and services on people's self-esteem and worth.

Not everyone depends on these donor due diligence websites. More donors are doing their own research to learn about your organization. According to one survey, the percentage of donors who usually do research on their own before giving for the first time or renewing their gift has increased from 59% to 78% over a seven-year span.[14]

The Chronicle of Philanthropy reported the following:

"Most potential supporters researched nonprofits by viewing charities' websites — and just under 42 percent of those people decided not to give after viewing them." One of their top reasons for not giving: "They saw little evidence of measurable results from donor contributions..."

Researching a nonprofit is popular among Millennials givers. One recent survey claimed 96% of them research an organization, compared to 88% for Gen X.[15] That's a pretty high research rate for both generations. It's not that they don't trust the donor due diligence websites. It's because, as mentioned, those websites don't provide the kind of information they care most about, which is clear, tangible results.[16]

Finally, a Fidelity report on the future of philanthropy makes this significant prediction: "Over time, the number of people who will make a donation without researching nonprofits will continue to shrink."[17] Indeed, the report states how small and mid-level donors are beginning to behave like philanthropists. And researching those organizations will have much to do with knowing the degree of impact their gift can have.

3.

Impact Stories = Your Narrative

Sometimes wisdom comes from unexpected places. Writing for Outside magazine, Pulitzer prize-winning author Nicholas Kristof argued, "For charities to prove their worth, they should write stories about individual empowerment, individual hope, and the promise that donors can make a difference in someone's life."[18] He said charities should forget about "logical arguments" (quote marks his) and descriptions of needs. In other words, he is saying you should only talk about ultimate impact: lives changed.

Kristof is partially right. Stories about human impact are indeed important ways to begin your presentation and frame results. They engage your audience. Stories can create empathy and generate compassion. A good ending can lead to action. People want to be involved in a success story, but just telling a good story about human change is not quite enough.

Well-formed stories alone can't provide potential donors with enough insight to know if they should invest in your organization. Organizations need clarity about what they expect to achieve. They must have well-defined strategies to accomplish their organization's goals. Finally, they need discipline to apply their methods while making adjustments as they learn.

Without clarity, focus, and discipline, it's hard for nonprofit organizations to produce consistent qualitative impact. No impact, no stories. No stories, no marketing strength. It's not circular thinking. It's logical thinking.

Capability produces impact and impact provides story content. The logical arguments Kristof believes you should eschew in favor of good stories are what generate success stories. These things are part of your story too. They form the backbone of your narrative, describing who you are, the genius of your methods, and what you accomplish because of it.

With faith-based organizations, the backbone of their narrative is often the *God-stories* that are surely there if their work is effective. Indeed, the notion of *spiritual metrics* is receiving more attention these days.[19] Figuring out how to observe, record, and talk about the spiritual impact your organization is producing has become increasingly necessary. This is how faith-based organizations can build more credibility among people who give to these kinds of organizations. You can't capture the God-stories using only numerical data and statistics.

Social sector nonprofits don't talk about spiritual metrics. Even so, the backbone of their narrative should still be phenomena change in people as a result of their services. The Harvard University authors of Entrepreneurship in the Social Sector said it well, admitting that directly measuring inputs, outputs, and activities don't always get to the most important things. Social sector organizations have to look for other indicators more closely linked to the *phenomena* they are trying to examine.[20]

Who Is Telling Your Story?

Whether you realize it or not, there is a narrative about your organization on the Web. Powerful search engines make it easy for donors to find that story. It's usually woven together through multiple websites. The information may come from your communication department on your official website. The narrative is also pieced together from unofficial sites, such as social media outlets or blogs written by staff, friends, and critics.

Potential donors are researching you. Third-party reviewers like Give Well are piecing together information about your organization. What story does this piecemeal Web search tell about your organization? Is it the story you want them to find, or worse, will your story turn them away?

Granted, you can't control everything people say, nor should you try. There is value in creative freedom that can benefit your organization. Still, unless you know what your narrative is and how to communicate it effectively, you are at the mercy of the uncontrolled freelance crowd.

It sounds like an impossible undertaking to produce an organizational narrative that has broad appeal. How can you possibly message to such a diverse population? Should you even try? To answer these questions, let's review your potential audience(s). Who are they?

Donors from the empire builder and baby boomer generations generally value truth and integrity. Just doing what you said you would do in practices and outcomes goes a long way with these two groups. They trust organizations based on legacy practices. They operate on shared assumptions with the organizations they support. Many Baby Boomers use the internet to gather information, so they are increasingly aware of change in the world.[21] They are also utilizing social media at a surprising level. Therefore, your narrative may be losing their interest at a faster rate than you think.

Gen Xers, the baby boomers' children, are entrepreneurial and innovative. They made their money fast as opposed to inheriting it. They expect funding recipients to also be fast, innovative, entrepreneurial, and effective.

Millennials—born after 1985—are a new breed, entirely.[22] They expect short time frames, rapid loops, lean startups, group creative processes, clear causes, risk taking, and addressing pressing problems with tangible solutions. They don't mind failure, as long as it is cheap and moves learning forward. And as mentioned, they are very big on research.

Clearly, knowing your donor audience has become more complex. Indeed, mission and social enterprise these days is more complex. However, now there is a new donor demographic emerging. It describes people from different generations who share one central concern: what is changing because of your service or ministry? A vague intangible answer will not due. The questioners want answers having to do with measurable change in the spiritual and social realms.

In the faith sector, donors of all ages are less impressed with numbers these days, such as churches planted, people baptized, Bibles translated, films shown, and hands raised. It can all sound mind-numbing to them. Rather, they are asking about quality results. That is, what has your organization done to make people and their community better off? Indeed, the terms 'impact' and 'transformation' have become quite the buzzwords. What is behind this shift?

Culture shift has much to do with it. Discussing how people change, anthropologist Paul Hiebert noted three culture shifts over the last 100 years. If you were operating as a charity in the nineteenth century, your impact research would have focused on outward signs through behavioral change. So you would have reported that x number of people are no longer using vulgar language. They no longer drink, smoke or dance, at least not in the presense of other church members.

During the twentieth century, faith organizations focused more on helping people believe the right things, so the intangible goal of increased knowledge would have been your measurment focus.

Now faith and even social sector organizations are focusing more on deep-level transformation. And no surprise, deep, lasting change that happens in individuals and their community is what many donors now want to know. They also want to know how positive change will be sustained and even expand.

These days, high capacity and middle income level givers need more than a good story. They want to know your business model. That is, your plan to produce impact. Therefore, a one-off in-depth story, as good as it may be, doesn't provide the spiritual and social proof that donors increasingly desire. One story doesn't validate your work.

In fact, the single story may actually be the exception, rather than the norm. As Chimamanda Ngozi Adichie warned, it may even misrepresent reality for the impacted people. Instead, think impact stories on a broad scale. Capture enough stories to paint an accurate portrayal of people undergoing positive change.

Of course, it would cause confusion to report multiple stories in a single marketing piece. In fact, doing that goes against conventional wisdom. Advertising experts say you should focus on one story and one person who your audience can more easily identify with.

That may be true if you are trying to capture a person's attention leaving them with a positive impression of your organization. It may even produce a one-time gift. But for validating success, it's not enough. Your real success story—your narrative—is how you put two and two together, how that created a breakthrough, how your patient, painstaking process and hard-learned lessons were beginning to produce change on a broad scale. Now describing and reporting that change is the icing on the cake!

This is the kind of organization more donors want to be a part of today, yet they don't know about you this way because it's not how nonprofits typically market themselves. Instead, nonprofits have fallen into the trap of talking more about how wonderfully trustworthy they are. They go into great detail about how impressive their processes are without really proving how impressive they really are.

It's not about you or your organization. People know how good your organization is by the results of your work. Sadly, most organizations can't talk about their good results in clear and compelling ways because they don't spend time measuring and documenting the quality of that work. Their enduring faith in their processes coupled with untested assumptions carries them along. Not so much for the donors anymore. They need more.

No Need for False Levels of Precision

Darren Walker, President of the Ford Foundation, said something that should be reassuring for small nonprofit organizations. "The real and pressing importance of identifying and measuring progress toward outcomes is often conflated with…false levels of precision." He thinks precision is often oversold.[23]

Nonprofit organizations with small budgets either oversell impact or they don't try measuring impact at all because they assume they need to demonstrate precision. Yet according to Douglas Hubbard, author of *How to Measure Anything*, the most intractable intangibles are often measured by surprisingly simple methods.[24]

Hubbard explains how the concept of measurement naturally assumes a complicated rigorous method applying the right algorithm, and done in a way that suffices publication in a scientific journal. Yet in so many cases, an organization just needs to decrease its level of uncertainty about the kind of impact they are making. It's not about eliminating uncertainly entirely. As Walker suggests, that arouses suspicion about false levels of precision. Evaluating quality change does not need to be so precise if some level of ambiguity can be tolerated. Most people can live with some ambiguity, as Hubbard says.

This is all good news for a lot of nonprofit organizations who don't have the budget or expertise to prove effectiveness to the professionals. But don't shelve the idea of careful evaluation quite yet. It doesn't mean qualitative impact evaluation can be by-passed outright. It also doesn't mean an organization should settle for the easiest things to measure either.

If evaluation goals are for internal learning, then evaluate in a way that provides you with the kind of impact information you need most. This is meant to improve program design and implementation. If impact data needs to be credible for a funder, then produce enough documentation to show your own biases didn't interfere with your evaluation methods.

The assumed burden of providing precise credible impact reports are what keep many nonprofit organizations from attempting to do qualitative evaluation at all. Yet most donors and funders don't expect them to use large amounts of budget and time to provide empirical proof of the nonprofit's work. They just want enough evidence to show their funds are creating measurable spiritual and social value in the lives of people who have needs.

4.

What Qualitative Evaluation Is (and Isn't)

Outcome-oriented or result-oriented planning has been around for years. In simple terms, it means clearly defined goals with benchmarks and monitoring to ensure progress towards achieving desired outcomes.

Researching what an outcome or a result is with many nonprofit organizations is revealing. Outcome is usually defined as a thing produced, such as quality childcare, safe housing, a good school, job training, and improved access to healthcare. In the faith sector, outcomes are churches planted, people saved, audio recordings distributed, and training programs completed. These are all results that can be immediately observed and reported.

But when did outcomes become just something to be counted, rather than a benefit to be studied and understood? The culprit is the unspoken belief that producing things automatically creates change. We have undying faith in things we work so hard to produce. We're proud of the processes we have worked hard to develop. We believe processes and the things it produces will accomplish change. Hopefully it will, but is there still too much guess work?

Outcome-oriented planning has really been more about short-term intervention, although most agency leaders would disagree. They believe they are working for long-term change. Even so, their planning and execution operates as if they are working for an intervention. That's because their strategic focus is producing things that provide immediate, often temporary, solutions to problems.

To be fair, an organization's outcomes may not be on the level of urgent intervention, like saving women trapped in prostitution. Once an intervention is complete, the next step in outcome-oriented planning is to provide healing, education, and job training for the women so they don't end up back in prostitution.

Most people would call these things project outcomes, but it all still focuses on producing necessary things to achieve impact. If the project ended there, what would happen to the women later? We don't know because the organization didn't discuss that question from the beginning.

Results, Outcomes, and Impact

This section looks a little closer at *change models*. Meaning, how all of the resources and activities produce a changed situation.

Illustration 1 is a simple change model. It shows the linear steps for producing an outcome, the ultimate result of a process. A word about terminology will help here. It is quite ordinary for people to use the terms 'output', 'outcome', and 'impact' interchangeably to describe results. The four stages in this change model are defined by the examples in Table 1.

Illustration 1. Standard Change Model Planning

Table 1. Examples of Illustration 1 Terms

Inputs	Funding, human resources, material, equipment.
Activities	Training, coaching, building, guiding, advising, etc.
Outputs	Completed buildings, trained people, resources developed.
Outcome	Access to low income housing, avoiding HIV/AIDS, learning from Bible studies, reduction in human trafficking.

For our purpose here, Illustration 1 shows how organizations typically plan to produce an outcome. Each stage is meant to move the organization along until the result—the outcome—is achieved.

With this model, a results report—also called an outcome or impact report—would typically provide the number of women who have left prostitution and have completed a job training course. What happened to the women, their family, or their community as a result of the intervention? This is a qualitative question. It's where the *long-term change* part can be observed and understood.

Of course, outcomes need to be achieved for ultimate mission success. Results-based planning produces discrete steps in a logical order, but it shouldn't stop at outcomes. Impact is quality change stemming from the existence of outcomes, as Illustration 2 shows.

Qualitative impact is often a missing piece in program planning. This is because we plan for things we can count, not intangibles that cannot be captured well by counting.

If we care most about lasting quality change, planning should begin with a discussion on qualitative impact and then work backwards.

Indeed, beginning with a discussion around qualitative change affects the other areas in Illustration 2. For example, it sharpens understanding about outcomes that are most critical. It clarifies what outputs are most needed to achieve those outcomes, and so on.

Some people call this a reverse logic planning model, as shown in Illustration 2. It is reverse because it begins with an ultimate impact goal in mind and then works backward. This process produces more clarity on the sorts of resources (the inputs and outputs) most needed to be successful.

Illustration 2. Impact-Oriented Change Planning

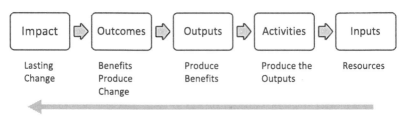

It's not that statistical descriptions of outcomes are no longer valued. It still is. However, these days, donors are also interested in the quality of change behind the numbers. That is, values added, problems solved, hope restored, dignity maintained, and situations reversed. How do you count these items? You don't, at least not at first. Your first step is to look for the impact you planned for and work to discover impact that actually occurs.

It's a Matter of Discovery

Qualitative impact evaluation usually begins with the question word, "why." Why is this high school girl getting such good grades now? Why is she running for class president? Why is this teenage boy going home after school to care for his younger siblings while his mother is at work? He used to avoid going home after school, leaving his younger siblings to fend for themselves. Why is this former homeless person in the U.S. raising funds for homeless street children in India?

These are examples of qualitative life-changes that happened as a result of an organization's services. To understand what changed, you also need to know from the start why these people needed the kind of help the programs offered. That is the baseline information used to measure success. Let's call it a "why baseline."

Why develop the why baseline data? It can be tedious work, and besides, you know what positive change looks like because you know the kind of people your organization serves. You can probably explain it well to anyone who asks about it. Even so, developing baseline data from the start is important for two key reasons.

First, you need to be able to demonstrate to other people, like an astute funding proposal reviewer, how your methods deliver impact. It's a result of your inputs and outcomes.

Secondly, having something concrete to compare results with is very helpful for your organization. Establishing links between impact and the process that led to it validates your methods. It's your proven change theory; the proof of concept. It shows a potential donor the likelihood of making a difference with their funding help.

This provides a persuasive talking point when facing the hard questions skeptics ask. Remember Live Safe's bad experience in the introduction? Being able to link children's improved education to sanitary water would have provided a satisfying answer to the reviewer's "so-what" question.

You may have preconceived notions of what success looks like, and that's okay. As anthropologist Paul Hiebert explained, "Humans search for coherence between the world as they see it and the world as we experience it. Humans seek meaning by looking for order, pattern, symmetry, coherence, unity, and non-contradiction." Yet, qualitative evaluation is often a matter of contradiction. That's because great impact happens in ways we don't always expect.

When studying the results of their work, Western Christian mission agencies working in non-Western contexts tend to look for Hiebert's patterns, symmetry, and non-contradiction in those results. That means they assume outward examples of impact will correspond with their world and experiences. They tend to overlook other people's rituals and customs affected by project outcomes. Therefore, they ignore or dismiss things that seem insignificant in their world that could be highly significant in the beneficiaries' world.

Impact often begins when a shift in thinking influences culture and rituals. For example, why did some women in India stop the practice of infanticide? Culturally, there are reasons why they terminate a new-born life and those reasons make sense to them, even as emotionally painful as it must be.

Along comes an organization dedicated to ending infanticide. Their education process helps the women and their husbands view life from a different perspective. They help them understand the value and dignity of all people created by God. Over time, many of the people they serve stop the practice. This is mission success.

A simple outcome report to the organization's donors may read: "This year 320 newly-married women and their husbands agreed to nurture their newborns, regardless of the gender." That is a wonderful intervention, but what else happened? The organization's leaders don't really know, yet this unknown is the area of impact they need to discover. It's what reveals the lasting change they and their donors work for.

What might they discover if they looked into things a bit deeper? Gender infanticide is generally foreign to their own Western culture. Therefore, they'd have to guess what is happening beyond their services. But guessing is not proof of their methods. They need more. A discovery process would look into what is changing in people and their culture. They could happily discover:

- Women and men are more at peace, having been freed from the traumatic prospect of ending a newborn's life.

- Marriage and economy that doesn't rely on gender is on the rise.

- Families are beginning to form alliances to only allow marriage between people who value both genders.

- Over time, cultural marriage practices will change until infanticide is no longer necessary or desired.

These are cultural transformations that take place over time. It is the mark of success for the organizations trying to end infanticide. At first, all they need to do is look for short-term evidence of change. These are the indicators that show their methods are beginning to work. It's the difference they are beginning to make and the answer to the "so-what" question a donor might ask.

This is why qualitative impact evaluation is largely about discovery. Certainly, there are predetermined key outcomes you still need to look for based on your change theory. Yet we don't tend to know if those things exist in very deep and broad ways. Additionally, we may find things that far surpass what we expected to find or things that fall short. We may also find things that challenge our own assumptions of what we think change is supposed to look like.

This kind of transparency is healthy for your organization. It is also viewed with admiration by most donors. When you start looking, you might be surprised to discover how the results of your services impact several areas of society.

Table 2 provides some general areas that could reveal important insights in how your organization is making an impact.[25]

Table 2. Impact Insights

Area	Impact Insight
Cause of Problems	New or improved solutions to deal with things such as sickness, famine, war, hopelessness, social disintegration, diseases, fear, trauma, human trafficking, homelessness, substance abuse.
Affected Relationships	People's relationships are improving and/or influencing change in extended family, kin, neighbors, cultural outsiders, community, enemies, etc.
Networks	People are bringing beneficial change to their economic, religious, institutional, and social settings.
Time/purpose	People are gaining a new understanding of their origins and reason for existence, resulting in changed behavior.
Social Solutions	People are bringing beneficial change to marriage, family, cultural expectations, placation, worship.
Forms of power	People are applying beneficial change in areas of male dominance, church, tribal, government, economic, conflict resolution.

Intangibles Can Be Measured

You need to measure intangibles if you want insights on long term change. Western development agencies still largely evaluate change in terms of physical change removed from what is happening in the spiritual or social realm. Cultural phenomenon that underlies responses to development efforts are not typically considered. Blame this on a dualistic Western Greek heritage. Physical and spiritual worlds form a stark dichotomy. Western agencies, being good Enlightenment thinkers, only consider material solutions apart from spiritual causation.

For example, a Western aid program seeks to convince Zambian women to have their babies in hospitals. So they offer them a blanket and a few other material goods if they agree to deliver in a hospital. The assumption is the women will discover how hospital deliveries are better, thus changing hundreds of years of cultural practices. But what are the cultural factors that influence Zambian women to not deliver in hospitals? It's not just a shortage of money. There are many reasons, and female infanticide is one of them.

Impact evaluation should look at what is changing on the inside, that is the negative cultural practices that are changing as a result of your work. Zambian women need to know their husbands won't abandon them if they only deliver female babies in the hospitals they are persuaded by Western agencies to utilize.

Testing Our Own Cherished Assumptions

The word 'assumption' has been used several times in this book. So much of what nonprofit organizations do is based on assumptions about outcomes and impact. If the organization has been around for a while, their assumptions are probably not time-tested. That is a problem. Even if their strategies are still generally effective, results will eventually diminish simply because the only constant you can bank on is that the world changes.

Funders also operate on assumptions. Some of them are beginning to question those operating beliefs. Clara Miller, President of the F.B. Heron Foundation put it this way, "Only by rigorously questioning and transcending our own cherished assumptions will we progress."[26]

For nonprofit organizations, the assumptions are always there. The question is whether or not you recognize them. Doing so is important for learning and growing. A good learning conversation is qualitative. What evidence is there to suggest your assumptions are either valid or invalid? Program improvements are based on more data with fewer assumptions, so the picture becomes clearer over time. The goal is to convert assumptions into working knowledge.

Chart 1. Predictive Assumptions

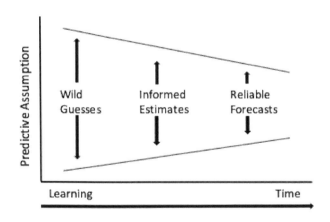

Impact evaluation reduces your level of uncertainty about the results of your organization's work. Are people really better off now that they have applied your discipleship training? Are women's lives improving because of job training? Is peace developing because of mediation?

Are people working their way out of poverty through micro-loans? Is the presence of a church bringing peace to a village?

If you have never done much in the way of impact evaluation, then your level of uncertainty is quite high. That means your assumptions about positive results could be wild guesses. Regularly assessing the impact of your work produces learning. Over time learning reduces your level of uncertainty. Now you can make informed estimates about impact.

As you keep assessing and learning, over time your level of uncertainty decreases even more. Now you can make reliable predictions about the results of your organization's work. The more predictable the outcomes, the lower the risk. Reducing risk makes you attractive to more donors.

5.

Planning for Qualitative Impact Evaluation

This chapter provides a brief overview on how to plan an impact evaluation. The goal is to get you started quickly by using some simple methods to collect the story data you need. As you apply these methods you will begin to discover what works best for you, understanding that you can make adjustments as you learn along the way.

Your Business Case

1. Describe Your Change Theory

Recall Illustration 2 in Chapter 4 describing the steps in producing transformational impact. When planning an evaluation, describe how your organization's model produces change. What are the steps you use to produce that change? Briefly list them so everyone can see the logical progression.

Begin with the end in mind by identifying your most important impact goals. This is what you will hold yourselves accountable to achieve. Then work to the right identifying the highest level to lowest level outcomes. Table 3 provides a simple example from an organization that works with HIV/AIDS orphans.

Table 3. Reverse Logic Change Model

Ultimate Impact	Important Outcomes	Important Outputs	Key Activities	Necessary Inputs
Reducing the number of orphans to zero by reducing HIV/AIDs among parents	Restoring and transforming people	Building Partnerships with services, schools, churches, and businesses	Working with AIDs families – social and spiritual training	Develop: • Financial partners • Service partners • Church partners • Civic partners

Notice the use of verbs in Table 3 examples, especially with impact and outcomes. These two categories are your key selling points for donors. So instead of describing an inanimate noun—those countable things—describe conditions and situations. These show the lasting and increasing value of your work. This is what people want to invest in; lasting growth in impact.

2. Explain What You Hope to Learn

Mario Morino, author of *Leap of Reason,* says evaluation isn't just to satisfy funders.[27] It's simply good practice for your organization. Learning over time improves decision-making. It makes you more effective at what you do.

What are the most important things you hope to learn? What areas of uncertainty do you want to reduce? Make a list of the most important questions you need to find answers to. But go into this with eyes wide open because, as organizational development expert Edgar Schein says, learning requires giving up something you know and are comfortable with.[28]

3. Justify the Cost

What is the value of new information? How can establishing a clear link between an activity and an outcome position your organization for greater results? What is the price of being more certain about your methods and processes? How much would you invest to provide better evidence of success for a donor or funding agency? Impact evaluation affirms the bottom line. It increases the value of your organization.

All of these things provide a return on investment when doing impact evaluation. If CFOs and other upper level leaders understand impact evaluation as their organization's return on investment, they shouldn't hesitate to allocate enough funds to do impact evaluation well.

Your first attempt at impact evaluation should be viewed as an experiment. This is because you don't have a track record for doing it well and cost-effectively yet. The goal of experiments and pilot projects is primarily meant for learning. Cost associated with learning is justifiable if you learn enough. Failure is okay if the lessons you learn moves things forward.

People in charge of spending need to see the cost as mission critical. Considering the cost apart from the benefits of impact measurement doesn't tell you anything about the cost-benefit ratio. If they say, "We can't afford impact measurement," then the question must be asked, "What is the cost of not doing it?"

4. Establish a Baseline for Comparison

A baseline is simply a description of the situation before your organization began to apply your services. It describes the situation your organization wants to change. Results from doing impact evaluation are compared to the baseline to see what has changed.

For example, you described students' condition upon admission to an after-school program. That is their academic performance, attitudes, view on life, view of God, relationships, etc. One year later, impact evaluation seeks to know what has changed in these areas? Establish direct links between program activities with positive (or negative) changes.

Table 4. Baseline Examples

Baseline (Before)	Change (After)	Cause of Change
Negative view of life	Positive view of life	Bible Studies
Poor grades	3.5 GPA	Tutoring
Few friends	Several healthy friendships	Group community service
Low self-esteem	Ran for High School class president	Counseling

Impact Measurement Methods

For some time now, measurement and evaluation has applied a scientific process of sorts. The method asked people to answer multiple choice questions. A Likert scale was used to capture the more abstract range of experiences from least to most. Another method asked those being surveyed to rank in order what was most true. It narrowed complicated questions to a simple yes or no answer. At times open-ended questions were asked. Focus groups of peers or dissimilar people provided answers to standardized questions.

There are challenges in collecting reliable qualitative data with these methods. For example, there are barriers to candid feedback, such as the feeling that you are being tested, the abstract scientific questions used, response bias favoring project leaders or funders, and with group interviews, bandwagon bias.

While these survey methods may provide some helpful information, they are not that useful in seeking evidence for transformational change in people. It's not that qualitative evaluation is anti-science. It's just that the scientific methods described above don't provide clear links to situations, patterns, and conditions that help you understand what is changing and why it is changing. It doesn't ensure the respondents understand the questions or the choices they must choose when providing a response.

The Data Is in the Dialogue

Over the last decade, survey experts have questioned how reliable standardized interview and focus group methods are. As survey experts Suchman and Jordan put it, "The questionnaire designer attempts to control not only what gets talked about in the interview, but precisely how topics get talked about as well."[29] In a way, it predetermines what the answers should be. It disrupts normal conversational behavior. This calls into question the validity of the data you collected, says psychologist Judith Tanur.[30]

The people your organization serves have a difficult time answering direct survey questions like, "Tell me about the kind of impact you have experienced in this project." Even simple requests like, "Tell me how this project has affected you" or "What changes have you made because of this project," may be met with blank stares.

There are reasons why this line of questioning is not very effective. The questions lack context. They are disembodied from a conversation. They ask for abstract information and analysis. They treat the person in an impersonal way as simply a source of data. Finally, they implicitly communicate that you are expecting them to provide answers you will like. It puts pressure on them to deliver, once they figure out what you are trying to get at.

Gaining insights on program results requires collecting qualitative data in the form of testimonies, stories, admissions, and opinions through *open dialogue* between researcher and interviewee.

Talk *with* People

Instead of plying interviewees with rigid standardized questions, the survey experts mentioned recommend you actually *dialogue* with them. That means you need to discuss your questions with the people you are interviewing so you can clarify and elaborate. In a way, they help you design good questions that help them understand what you want to learn from them.

This process depends on natural, informal, open dialogue with the interviewee to discover their change stories. That means who talks and who controls the dialogue is shared between interviewer and interviewee.[31] This approach is more suitable for oral cultures in which oral learning and oral communication of religious and social values is the norm.

This may not sound 'scientific' but that is okay. Dialogue, rather than formal interview, should help us understand their experiences. It gives us a closer view of real-life situations. This can be achieved better by dialogues that reveal change which may not surface when following standardized questionnaires. So in this case, research is two directional interaction rather than one-way interviews.[32]

It's a Spiritual Thing

Impact evaluation through dialogue probes spiritual or phenomenon issues. That is why a qualitative approach is necessary. You are trying to make observations in the real world. Therefore, a dialogue approach doesn't just ask "how" questions, rather "what" questions. What is changing and what is not changing? You need to interpret what you hear.

This could lead to "why" or "why not" questions. For example:

"What happened when the church members began using the new Bible translation?"

"They developed a deeper understanding about Jesus and his teachings."

"Has anything changed now that they understand Jesus' teachings?"

"Men are treating their wives better."

"Why would knowing Jesus' teaching cause them to do that?"

"They understood that God is against people who mistreat others, especially a spouse. They want God's blessing in their lives, so this seemed like a way to receive that."

For another example:

> "*Have you observed any differences with the people who finished the training courses.*"
>
> "*Yes.*"
>
> "*Great. What are some of those differences?*"
>
> "*The people who successfully finished the courses are behaving differently now. In fact, when you walk down the street in their village, you can easily pick out where the training participants live.*"
>
> "*What makes them stand out?*"
>
> "*Their yards are cleaner. There's no garbage scattered around. Their children are more well-kept and clean.*"
>
> "*Do you know why they are like that now?*"
>
> "*I think it's because they have self-esteem now. They have hope now. They are more optimistic about their future.*"

These are examples of phenomenon or spiritual change stemming from an outcome of learning and self-improvement. It is the ultimate lasting impact you work for. But it's intangibly hidden, so dialogue tends to bring the transformation stories out.

It's a Social Thing

For an example of social impact, how would you dialogue with recipients of a microfinance loan? Microfinance is a means to help the poor attain loans to start businesses and open savings accounts. This helps them improve their lives by slowly working their way out of poverty. In 2014, microfinance loans totaled 10 billion dollars globally.

Being freed from poverty is a significant accomplish that would certainly count as success for a microfinance organization. Yet there must be significant stories about what happened with families and villages once they started climbing out of their impoverishment. For many people, this is what nonprofits strive for, yet without enough case studies and stories describing what economic progress produces, it's still just counting outcomes.

You could track loan repayment, business growth, and savings account growth. These kinds of statistics would be informative, but it doesn't get at the heart of impact. One microfinance organization tracks physical improvements to houses, better drinking water, toilet facilities, and a source of lighting as impact indicators.[33] These are good indicators that the loans are improving the recipient's quality of life.

But how are their lives changing? Are people moving from poverty to adequacy? Being freed from poverty produces dignity. What is dignity producing? How does better health and business ownership affect their children's future? What is their general outlook on life now? How is an improved outlook influencing choices they make? How is their community beginning to benefit?

This is the transformational impact of microfinance loans. These kinds of stories really capture ultimate success. It goes beyond the intervention stage to document the resilient stage of human physical and spiritual progress. The stories are there. You just need to discover them. Using a dialogue method can help.

How to Dialogue Effectively

Having a conversation doesn't mean the survey lacks structure to get the information you need. You do prepare initial starter questions. Follow-up questions have a purpose. If the conversation is not providing insights, there are strategies to refresh the discussion. This section provides tips on planning and holding dialogues with program beneficiaries. Chart 2 shows the process of conducting surveys through dialogue style interviews.

Chart 2. Dialogue Process

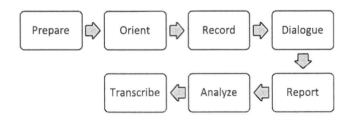

Prepare

Although the goal is to have ordinary conversations, you still need to prepare questions before the dialogues begins. These are starter questions about a topic you need to understand. They are not standardized questions that must be asked in the same way with each person. You will likely refine the questions or ask new ones based on responses during the conversations. Remember, the goal is not rigid analysis, rather discovery that provides important insights.

Dialogue Partners

Conversing with individuals and small groups is desirable. Groups tend to create synergy in the discussion, assist with collective memory, and add components to the story they are telling. Individuals may share more private information.

Before launching into a conversation, help your dialogue partner understand the process. Ask them if they have any questions before starting. Reassure them whatever they say is helpful. Encourage them to speak from the heart, and remind them they are not being tested for anything.

Audio / Video Recording

If permitted and possible, someone other than the interviewer should make an audio or video recording of the conversation in a way that doesn't distract the people being interviewed. Later on, listen to the recordings of the dialogue sessions. You don't necessarily need to produce a word-for-word transcription, which can take hours. Rather, just take notes on the *themes* being discussed to capture the most significant parts of the dialogue.

Dialogue Methods

The goal of the dialogue is to understand how a project (or topic) influenced the interviewee's life in specific ways. It can be anything at all they would like to talk about. The following provides some methods to produce fruitful conversations.

- Use Warm-Up Questions

    This helps them understand what you want to know. Use ordinary conversation, not forms or prepackaged-sounding questions that you ask. It needs to sound like natural conversation to the interviewee and not a test that requires a "correct" answer.

- Use Your Prepared Questions to Start

    But if the questions are not working, don't keeping repeating them. Instead, redesign them on-the-fly.

- Circling Back

  Use follow-up questions to circle back to something you heard that reveals useful information pertaining to your topic, whether it is positive or negative.

- Ask for Clarifications

  If the response to a question is cursory, vague, ambiguous, or the questioner simply wants to hear more, they can ask the respondent to say more.

- Don't Hint

  If you're seeking confirmation on something you already suspect, ask objectively and directly. Don't hint, as if fishing for the right answer.

- Don't Ask Leading Questions

  That presumes they must provide an answer you will like, such as "Did you like the way the training course was conducted?"

- Ask Short Questions

  Long complicated questions are difficult for even the smartest person to follow. Start with short, simple questions. Use a follow-up question to add more information.

- Avoid Loaded Terms

  Loaded terms are judgmental words. These are words that communicate a bias, like "fortunately," "wonderful," or "obviously." A response may be influenced by such words.

- Establish Common Ground

    Judith Tanur explains how establishing common ground with your dialogue partner can be divided into two areas. There is cultural common ground and personal common ground.
    If you are working with people from a different culture, you may need to look for personal common ground. Establishing common ground reduces tension and opens up more natural dialogue because you *get each other* on a certain level. Cultural common ground can develop because of shared experiences in religious, social, and professional experiences.[34]

- Help People Remember

    Like all of us, over time we begin to forget the details of an experience. The more distant the experience, the more help we need to remember those details. Before asking a question, help the interviewee remember by establishing some benchmarks.
    For example: "When the literacy classes concluded, the students all received certificates of course completion. Then you all went back to your home area. Do you remember how your neighbors welcomed you back? How did they respond to your new status as a female literate person?"
    Before starting a dialogue, the interviewer can provide a list of events for the interviewee to look over. This will jog their memory, and then your detailed questions will have a recovered context for them to draw from.

Analyzing the Data

If you gather enough impact story data through multiple conversations, you can place the impact themes in a table to see what patterns and trends emerge. You can see what sort of impact is most significant to least significant. You might identify impact gaps you were not expecting. This is where your quantitative measures show how broad or significant certain trends may be.

Table 5 provides a simple example of how the aggregation of stories generated from dialogue paints a picture of program success. What change items would emerge from your dialogue interviews? What measure of organizational goals would be reflected in your table?

Be aware that placing outcomes and impact into categories is subjective and can affect results. The idea is to try and observe common patterns in certain areas that may elevate those areas as more significant.

Table 5. Frequency of Change

Kinds of Change	Frequency	Program Service
Better relations with neighbors	35	Community service training
More peace in the village	38	Conflict mediation
Children are healthier	27	Health education
More hopeful for the future	31	Spiritual training
Taking charge of our lives	17	Family counseling

Doing impact evaluation through open, natural dialogue includes more affected people in the research, and it gives them a greater voice. Holding this sort of dialogue with many people combines multiple voices. From their stories you should be able to observe patterns or trends developing because of your organization's activities.

It is a repetitive process. Each time you dialogue with a program beneficiary, you gain another piece of the picture. Each story increases understanding. Now you have more insight, which produces more insightful questions. The dialogue goes deeper and better information emerges.

The combined story data provides valuable information for program staff. They will have a better understanding about how the programs they carry out are working. It will also reveal gaps and weak areas that need to be addressed.

You will also have the sorts of stories, testimonies, and admissions donors are keenly interested in hearing. They will be happy to know about trends developing, which show increasing impact over time. It's their ROI.

The Art of Case Studies

Simply stated, a case study is a single study that seeks to understand impact in generalized ways within one community or across a number of communities.[35] It seeks to describe cases that now exist because of your organization's work. Case studies collect data on personal experience, self-analysis, life stories, interviews and cultural narratives.

The process relies much on observing changes. It puts together pieces of recent history to help understand what has changed. However, it's not just about observing things. It relies on interactions with people associated with the project and even some more distant from the project.

The people doing a case study gather data through observation and dialogue often in story form because people like to tell stories about their experiences. Don't worry about scientific objectivity. Case study requires you to interpret what you are observing and learning. After forming these interpretations, you will probably modify or even replace questions with follow-up studies. That is okay. The case study process is meant to provide deeper insights, which leads to better questions producing better dialogue.[36]

The easy thing about case studies is that it doesn't necessarily follow certain theories. In fact, experts say case studies often end up revealing some flawed assumptions a researcher brings to the study.[37] This means doing case study requires humility when confronted by data that is counter to a researcher's own biases and assumptions.

For example, traditional Western Church survey methods tend to follow preconceived ideas of what impact is in their own Western contexts, and then researchers seek to confirm those things in non-Western settings. However, case studies are meant to discover and describe local reality on local terms, as best we can. We can anticipate that some of our cherished assumptions and theories will be proven false. This, too, is the goal of case studies.

Robert Stake, author of The Art of Case Study Research, said "Much of our gathering of data from other people will take the form of stories they tell and much of what we convey to our readers will preserve that form."[38] So even though you have to interpret the data, the raw stories should be shared widely, so others can interpret that data.

Table 6. Case Study Strengths and Weaknesses[39]

Strengths	Weaknesses
Provides depth of understanding.	Selection bias may overstate or understate relationships of cause and effect.
Validates conceptual assumptions of impact.	Weak understanding of occurrence in population of phenomena under study.
Shows understanding of context and process.	Statistical significance unknown or unclear in the wider context.
Understanding of what causes a phenomenon, linking causes and outcomes.	Small random samplings may not be representative.
Fosters new cause-effect correlations and improved research questions.	Subject to researcher bias

Because you have to interpret story-based data, some people may complain the study is too prone to researcher biases, and that may be true. So when producing a report of the case study you conducted, avoid talking in terms of objective facts.

The case study provides deeper understanding of the situation your organization addresses. You learned a lot about cause and effect. You changed some of your assumptions and recognized interpretive biases. Freely admit those things, but also describe what you did learn and what your organization will do differently because of the study. This should disarm the critics who think only objective scientific rigor can produce reliable insights.

Community Participation

In her book Working with Stories, Cynthia Kurtz recommends including more of the affected people in the impact study. The experts call this participatory narrative inquiry (PNI). It involves groups of people from the affected community who help gather raw stories detailing their own beliefs, feelings, and experiences around a project.[40]

If you need to understand about social taboos and stigmas that can have significant influence on your project practices, then PNI provides a way to gain insights into those areas. The idea is to ensure the beneficiaries' stories, which can be suppressed when applying a more rigid survey method, are heard.

Table 7. Participatory Narrative Inquire Process[41]

Story Collection	Community members tell stories about their concerns and reactions to your organization's project, program, or intervention. The stories need to be collected in some way. Usually, someone is appointed to gather the stories.
Making Sense of the Stories	The community participants need to discuss the stories; to negotiate what it means so they can make sense of it from a community standpoint. This forms the basis of the impact report first draft.
Return	The community needs an opportunity to review what the final report says. They may want to correct it or modify it. This makes the report valid in their eyes since it represents their voices.

PNI is an open approach to impact evaluation. The goal is to capture many community voices. This is not a top-down method which could feel more coercive, thus producing unreliable data. If you really want to get at the heart of impact, both positive and negative, PNI can deliver the raw data.

When doing interviews, Kurtz encourages story gatherers to be sure to include a good mix of the affected people. In her terms, be sure the high and mighty, the downtrodden, the little kids, older folks, and peers are included.

Finally, don't under estimate the value of reporting community members' raw stories to donors and funders. As noted in Chapter 6 on marketing your brilliance, most donors want to know about those stories, and not just rosy reports written by your fundraising staff. *Community voices confirm impact.* It provides a personal connection between the affected people and your donors.

To learn more about PNI see Cynthia F. Kurtz. 2014. *Working with Stories in Your Community or Organization. Participatory Narrative Inquiry. Third Edition.* Kurtz-Fernhout Publishing.

Discovering Stories of Change

Because qualitative impact evaluation deals with spirituality or phenomenology, finding out what impact is in terms of how program beneficiaries see it requires more of a discovery process. Western people working in non-Western regions naturally assume people are impacted spiritually in the same ways they are. There are certainly areas of our lives that are affected in the same ways. Yet so often the most significant form of impact appears to be the least significant to a cultural outsider, so we tend to ignore those things.

For instance, many cultures fear the spirit world, so their daily lives are impacted by that fear. Indicators that people are being liberated from fear may come in forms Western observers would not recognize.

- A Papuan woman now eats fresh fruits and vegetables during pregnancy because she no longer fears the taboo that forbids eating those items during pregnancy. As a result, her baby is born healthy, strong and survives.

- Rather than pacifying capricious harmful spirits in order to receive a good harvest, a Filipino farmer now looks to a compassionate God to provide for his daily needs.

- In Africa, chickens traditionally sacrificed to appease spirits are now used as an important protein source for the family.

Whether you believe spirits exist or not, people's fear of the spirit world can greatly influence your development projects. Western medical workers in West Africa told relatives of a deceased person who died from Ebola to not touch the body during funeral rituals. That would help them avoid contamination. The medical workers didn't understand that not touching the body in saying good-bye would offend the deceased person's spirit. That could cause serious problems for the living relatives. They feared that more than the virus.

Certainly the relatives need to stop touching the bodies of Ebola victims to prevent the disease from spreading, but not addressing the spiritual ramifications is self-defeating. They still believe they need protection from angry ancestor spirits for disrespecting the dead.

When asking for stories about impact, don't be surprised if people begin with some rather odd sounding and apparently unrelated topics. As Kurtz described it, when South Africa's apartheid system fell, a commission was setup to collect testimonies about how apartheid affected people. A university researcher asked a woman to tell him about how the system had affected her. She began by saying,

"There was this goat…" The surveyor recorded the story and then filed it away, marked as irrelevant.

Later on another researcher came across the interview. She went to ask the women more questions about the goat story. As it turned out, the story was filled with meaningful information about suffering under apartheid, couched in a story about her goat.[42]

In many cultures, people use metaphors to explain things, especially if they are discussing sensitive topics. These sorts of stories are highly significant, yet they often go unreported because a surveyor doesn't recognize the forms people use to discuss sensitive or emotionally-difficult information.

Most Significant Change Method

A variation on Kurt'z Participatory Narrative Inquire method is Davies and Dart's *Most Significant Change* method (MSC).[43] The idea behind MSC is to discover stories describing change that are the most significant for project beneficiaries.

The method collects stories of change in the same way it was described earlier. However, the method uses a more systematic approach in gathering as many change stories as possible in order to find significant patterns and trends. Staff field workers gather stories from their region or location. Each person transcribes and then summarizes the story content. Next they send their story summary data to a central location.

There, field supervisors comb through the stories to analyze the results. The supervisors work to identify stories they think are the most significant in terms of project outcomes and impact. If there is another level of leadership, like country level leaders, they receive the supervisor's reports and recommendations on which stories are most significant. After reviewing those reports, they send the most significant change stories to their fundraising department.

Importantly, each level provides an opportunity for the people who provided the stories or reports to comment on the reports before sending them to the next level. If this is done at each level, the change stories could be refined and clarified. It is also an important part of reflective practice because the story tellers are the source of the stories. Seeing the reports provides insights for them too. Feedback from staff confirms one another's analysis.

Table 8 from the MSC guide provides an overview of the collection and analysis process.

Table 8. Most Significant Change Process

1. Stories of Change Reported		
2. Collected by Local Field Staff 1	2. Collected by Local Field Staff 2	2. Collected by Local Field Staff 3
3. Sent to Region 1 Staff	3. Sent to Region 2 Staff	Sent to Region 3 Staff
4. Regions 1-3 Data Reviewed by Country Level Committee		
5. Final Reports Sent to Fundraising Department		

A Brief Introduction to Developmental Evaluation

Thus far, I've been generally uncharitable about scientific methods that "prove" results based mostly on standardized, controlled, routinized methods for doing impact evaluation. You don't necessarily need these methods, because by now experience has taught you that your methods, as messy and inconstant as they can be at times, are pretty effective. You just need to find the evidence to point to. That is why we have focused on dialogue to get at the heart of change.

Some nonprofit organizations have clear, consistent programs that are easy to evaluate. Things are generally predictable, so results are generally foreseeable. If something goes wrong, they can usually find out what and fix it. This is more typical of social sector services. But nonprofits who work for transformational and spiritual change to affect behavior don't have such simple processes. Theirs is a world of general complexity with shifting circumstances, changing attitudes, inconstancies, and unpredictability. Cheer up. There's an impact evaluation method just for you! It's a relatively new method called Developmental Evaluation (DE).

DE is a real-time, learning-oriented, feedback-based, and insight-driven approach to program design and early implementation of a program or initiative.[44] As the author of Developmental Evaluation describes it, DE is especially useful and attractive to social innovators. I would add that it's useful for any nonprofit who deals with complexity on a regular basis.[45]

Table 9 provides some differences between traditional evaluation and developmental evaluation.

Table 9. Evaluation Model Comparison

Traditional Evaluation	Developmental Evaluation
Proves and validates program models.	Supports innovation and adaptation models.
Manageable and stable situations.	Complex, dynamic environment.
Focus on effectiveness, efficiencies, and impact.	Exploration, trials, ongoing innovation results.
Outcomes for beneficiaries and participants.	For scaling impact over time.
Outcome-driven.	System change-driven.
Program design based on linear approaches.	Program design based on non-linear approaches.

So this sounds nice. You have a lot of flexibility in how you evaluate because your evaluation is adaptive to whatever situations you are encountering at any given time. For example, at first people were showing up for the training programs, but now a cultural problem has emerged preventing them from coming. Your evaluation questions will be along the lines of:

- How much do they understand about disease now?

- How can we continue to communicate important medical information now that they can't attend classes anymore?

- What measurable difference will their current level of understanding make?

- What will happen to the community if they are no longer learning about what spreads disease?

On another problem:

People who attend awareness training on human trafficking seem to have reached a plateau of understanding. How can we evaluate the results of their current level of understanding?

- Is it enough to make a difference?

- Are there knowledge gaps?

- What should be the next step?

In the faith-sector, church-planting activities have been curtailed because of threats from opposing religious leaders. Evaluation questions may be:

- How did the local church workers benefit from our presence?

- How would our absence affect their ongoing work?

- What methods would actually increase their success going forward?
- How do local church members view the opposition?
- What aspect of the opposition could actually force us to change our strategy?

With DE, ongoing impact evaluation is designed as a response to changing situations, and not so much as a report for donors. You do gather data to find out how things are going. But the primary purpose of that data is to improve results, adjust to a change, and grapple with a complex situation that has arisen.

Some agency leaders become like a deer in the headlights when situations suddenly change. They are indecisive about action. They allow problems to linger, sometimes to the point of no return. Planning DE from the start helps avoid inaction because of regular monitoring and feedback. Indeed, it can prevent serious problems from emerging because regular monitoring and feedback saw the problem coming.

Reporting DE Impact to Donors

Just because DE focuses on gathering impact data for day-to-day awareness, that doesn't mean you are off the hook in donor reporting. You still need compelling impact information in seeking additional funding or for maintaining current funding.

The good news is, there are financial partners who don't mind funding these sorts of projects. Some are drawn to them. Most of these donors still care much about the people and causes you are involved in, so they do like to know how the beneficiaries are doing. They are still interested in information that shows your cause is moving toward greater success.

Yet because you deal with so much complexity and unpredictability, your donor reports will sound different, no doubt. People who financially support these sorts of projects will typically buy-in to what you are doing and they will stay with you as long as you provide reassuring information. By reassuring, I mean information that demonstrates learning with adjustments, which lead to improvements and overcomes obstacles. But don't stop there.

Keep it human, if humans are the beneficiaries. Include the stories of change referred to earlier. Show how people are increasingly better off because of your rapid learning, agility, and innovation. That is why most people are in this with you, even if the former part is thoroughly interesting to you.

Resource

Michael Quinn Patton. 2011. *Developmental Evaluation. Applying Complexity Concepts to Enhance Innovation and Use.* New York: The Guilford Press.

6.

On Marketing: How to Message Your Brilliance

They still don't understand what exactly your organization works to achieve. They've read the material on your website. They've watched the videos. They have seen your brochures. They have ideas about the sorts of things your organization does, yet they still don't understand what exactly your organization exists to accomplish. There is too much information for them to sort through.

One nonprofit organization in Southern Africa was often mistaken as a Christian ministry that helps African children in orphanages, whereas they were actually about preventing AIDs orphans from having no choice but to live in orphanages. How could they be so misunderstood?

It was because of their complicated message. They didn't simply and directly say they exist to provide AIDs orphans with a physically, emotionally, healthy alternative to forced-living in an over-crowded, impersonal orphanage. They could have said AIDs orphans in their alternative program outperform non-orphans academically and socially. Instead, their messaging content described various programs, partnerships, processes, methods, and procedures. The brilliance of their mission wasn't up front and identifiable. It was lost in the details.

This is one reason why most people who visit a website won't make a gift. Reading complicated material about processes and methods doesn't hold a first-time website visitor for more than a few seconds.

This is known as a bounce rate. It's happens when people navigate away from a website after only viewing the first page. A high bounce rate of 70% is not good. It means, only 30% click on something to learn more. An 80% bounce rate indicates a poor performing website. This is not uncommon behavior for donors who view marketing materials. Simply put, nonprofit messaging is too complicated.

Because outcomes have been associated with producing countable things for so long, nonprofit leaders, especially founders, love talking about how they produce those outcomes. It's like a factory manager explaining how they produced so many widgets that year. They are proud of the method they developed. They love the complexity that has increased over time because they understand it so well. They've become rather enamored with it all, and that is understandable.

There is nothing wrong with pride of ownership. But focusing on your complexity isn't necessarily going to attract today's givers. Potential donors may not care so much about those details. They are impressed with your results.

When making a face-to-face funding appeal or speaking at a fundraising event, nonprofit presenters tend to spend a lot of time talking about their organization, the goals they set, the activities they carry out, their mission model, etc. It's all about them.

They believe if they can impress you with all of the information, then you will make a gift. They add more information to those talking points, so presentation content gets rather bloated. Over time, they've created a complicated, inconsistent way to talk about their agency, both internally and externally. Most of the time, it all misses the most important point a donor or funder wants to know. It's the so-what test. What difference is it all making?

A venture capitalist who provides significant nonprofit funding said, if he can't tell what an organization ultimately accomplishes in the first few lines of a funding proposal, he moves on to the next proposal. If he understands mission impact in the first few lines, then he moves on to next paragraph to learn how they accomplish their impact. If he completes reading the first page, he's usually sold on their request for funds.

The truth is, so many proposals never get past the first few sentences. Your website homepage, YouTube video, tag line or brochure is your first few sentences.[46] You need to nail it down fast.

To avoid the so-what test, the goal is to generate a wait, what? question. For example, when someone asks what your mission is about, you respond with, "Our goal is unmanageable missions." Expecting a predictable jargon-filled answer, this response surprises them and arouses their curiosity. So they ask what you mean. Now you have their attention.

What You Say – What They Hear

Do your marketing pieces implicitly tell donors that you do the real work and they just provide funding for that work? It's as if providing funds isn't an important strategic role or spiritual ministry in its own right. Most donors can see right through it. Historically, they've been patient with that false view, but times are changing (See Gravelle 2014).[47]

As mentioned earlier, even lower and mid-level donors are beginning to act like philanthropists, and these emerging philanthropists are becoming more strategically engaged in the organizations they support. The parents and grandparents of these donors gave out of a sense of obligation and tradition, so they were indeed patient over one-way conversations with organizations they supported. Not so for the Gen X and Millennial givers. They see themselves as driven by values, strategy, and impact.[48] So treating them simply as funders of your work will not move them to the next page of your website or the next paragraph in your funding proposal.

Robert Rose and Carla Johnson, authors of *Experiences: The 7th Era of Marketing*, say forget about the sales funnel; your marketing steps. It is no longer relevant and brands no longer guide customers in their journey. Instead, companies need to know their customers better, because you can't create customer experiences that are relevant for them if you don't know them.[49]

I believe this also applies to fundraising, perhaps more so than commercial sales. Traditional measures used to persuade people to support your cause were like trying to get them to buy a product. But people don't want to be marketed to anymore, especially with nonprofit causes. They'd rather have a positive experience in connecting with your organization and cause.

In the past, nonprofit messaging has made broad statements to potential donors, like "You will know the difference you are making for your kids in Africa." This strategy assumed donors didn't care about what the difference is. If they thought somehow they were making a difference, then they were satisfied. It's a shallow experience.

Instead, state up front exactly what the difference will be in the children's lives, knowing that is just the beginning of a donor's giving journey with your organization. Knowing the *kind* of impact they can make is a big first step.

Rose and Johnson say, "Instead of trying to force people into the next step of a complex process that we've created, we must create experiences that are so mesmerizing and valuable that buyers want to take the next step, and then we make it obvious what that next step could be." It's very good advice for donor development as well.

What a Giving Journey Looks like

When you market your cause, think long-term engagement with donors and funders. They know you are investing in them, and that's not a bad thing. Author Ken Stern takes nonprofits to task for offering short-term gratification with minimal personal impact when seeking one-time spontaneous gifts.[50] Instead, Eden Stiffman, writing for *Chronicle of Philanthropy*, says fundraisers should focus their attention on getting donors involved in ways that lead to substantial gifts over the long term.[51]

Indeed, nonprofits tend to market themselves to make donor's "feel good" about their work, rather than make them value what their organization does. There is a difference, says Jason Saul.[52] He thinks talking about the good you do isn't good enough these days. You need to sell the impact your organization creates. Meaning, if a high capacity donor really values the impact your organization creates, they see their giving as investing in that impact.

Donors will more likely look at what your organization produces in terms of value rather than just effectiveness. Lower level givers would value the impact of their giving that much more, and this can lead to larger gifts. This is different from giving a gift because they feel good about what you do. Viewing impact this way can produce a profound shift on how you talk about your organization's results and how donors talk about your organization with others.

Julie Dixon and Denise Keyes, writing for Stanford Social Innovation review, make a very important point about donor advocacy.

> "As our research shows, organizations basically get what they ask for. Ask only for financial donations, and that is what people will think is their deepest level of involvement. But ask for more—sharing on social media, forwarding e-mails to friends, advocating for the organization, organizing and leading fundraising

events—and a person's contributions, as well as her sense of having an impact, can grow exponentially."[53]

In a giving journey, donors first learn about the kind of impact they can help produce, so they make a contribution. Subsequent donor reports send them further along the same uncomplicated, consistently-worded journey. Now they are learning a little more about the actual rather than theoretical impact of their gifts.

Their trust increases because you are transparent about good results and honest about the failures, which you openly shared in your report. They are ready to move further by giving again or increasing their giving. Or they may begin encouraging friends to give to your cause because they have a positive experience to share. As a result, some of their friends give to your organization. This produces a deeper sense of satisfaction for the donor, because now they've leveraged their financial impact through their friends.

Over time the donors want to go further, so they offer to advocate for your cause. They want to present your work to potential funders. Or they may invite you to present to an advocacy meeting they organize. It is difficult for development workers to gain access to inner circles, but advocates can help. By this point, your donor/advocate doesn't feel like just a donor. They feel like they are a part of your organization's cause.

To make their journey smooth and fulfilling, Table 10 describes things that can enrich a donor's experience. Starting at the top, each experience moves them along their journey with your cause in increasingly satisfying ways. However, this is about shared experiences with the organization, with their leaders, and with others. It's not about leading them to a predetermined destination. Ultimately, they need to chart their own path as they grow in their experience with your organization. You set the table by providing the kind of information that helps *them* do that best.

Table 10. Donor Experience and Journey

Experience	Journey
Shared Values	Talk about real impact that's important for them, not just theory.
Easy Path to Learning	Keep messaging content simple, clear, and consistent across all communication channels.
Valuing Their Time	Ask about the kind of communication they desire, e.g., print, email, text, tweet, Facebook, FaceTime, YouTube channel, Instagram, etc.
Feeling Valued	Ask for feedback on the usefulness of the reports you send them.
Feeling Resourceful	Ask your donors and funders how they would explain your cause to others.
Co-creation / Advocacy	Invite them to co-design a method for sharing your mission with friends.
Going Deeper	New insights in learning and vision building trips.
Informing Org. Strategy	Participation in leadership meetings to provide a donor/advocate point of view.

Reporting Impact Results

You know how to report impact and general results to your donors through your communication channels. What things do your reports cover? That is the subject of this section.

The areas you need to cover may surprise you because they are not what nonprofits typically report. But if you want to build deeper relationships with current and potential funding partners for the long term, then these areas will strengthen that relationship and increase trust.

Display Innovative Thinking

To increase impact, if not just break even on impact from year to year, organizations need to continually innovate. The simple reason is the world continually changes. Circumstances change. The more information becomes widely accessible the faster change happens. As a result, people's values also change. Strategies that were effective three years ago may already be losing effectiveness.

For an organization to remain effective, thus attractive to donors, you must demonstrate that you understand the latest thinking on the cause you are working for. Keeping your financial partners up to date on your latest thinking demonstrates that you aren't becoming irrelevant. Table 11 provides examples of innovative shifts from former methods to new methods.

Table 11. Innovative Shifts

Previous Method	New Method
Individual learning programs	Group learning programs
Print material	Oral – audio material
Limited partnerships	Broader impact partnerships
Training in town	Training where needs are greatest
Linear service delivery	Non-linear service delivery
Working with orphanages	Working with extended families of orphans
Logic tools for impact assessment	Story-based learning

Talk About Your Experiments

Innovative thinking leads to experimentation. You try something new and it sort of fails. But if you learn something important, then you are better positioning your organization for greater success. You have moved the needle on remaining effective, thus relevant. So share information on your experiments with donors. Highlight what you gained and also what didn't work. Tell them what you learned in the process and what will change because of it. Even small incremental improvements based on experiments are valuable.

For example, you decided to provide a meal for the poor before starting the micro finance training program each day. As a result, they payed closer attention to the program, which increased learning. You learned that many of them don't eat in the morning before coming to the training course. Feeling nourished improved their attention span. So now you make sure they are nourished before each training day. It's a simple change, but it made a significant difference. Now tell your financial partners about this in your next report.

Share Program Design

Capture the impact of your innovative designs. What are you doing that is uniquely designed to accomplish your mission? International Sanctuary works in India. They help women who have been rescued from human trafficking. There are several organizations that help women such as these make jewelry they can sell. But International Sanctuary's approach is unique.

They are about restoring these women's lives, helping them see themselves as God sees them—worthy, dignified, beautiful and strong. Making jewelry is actually a method that helps them see their creativity and inner beauty. That milestone opens their minds to greater potential. They develop their business, open a bank account, pursue higher education, and become financially independent. Yet it all begins with making a beautiful piece of jewelry they can sell.

Talk about what is beginning to change because of your organization's creative designs. How will that positive change increase? Even if you are only seeing small incremental impact happening as a result of your innovation, funders will still be impressed. It means you are not going to allow your mission to stagnate. That makes your organization an attractive place to give.

Using Your Quantitative Data in Reporting

Reports should be meaning-driven. That is, data that doesn't produce insights is really just a collection of facts and statistics. Recall Live

Safe's presentation in the introduction to this book. The presenter's data didn't offer any insights as to why those numbers were significant. Quantitative data only tells you how much. It doesn't tell you why. Even so, describing impact without figures showing how widespread the impact is doesn't help either. A credible report includes the quality and the quantity.

The next section provides some examples of how to use numerical and statistical information to explain facts in simple ways.

Report Stories of Change

This is the central part of your report. It shouldn't be long and complicated; however it should provide more depth than a few anecdotes. The stories you collected, the interviews you conducted, the listening you did when the group discussed how your work helped them; this is evidence that shows you are making a difference and what that difference is.

When doing impact evaluation, gathering enough samples usually reveals patterns and themes. This is because people who live in the same context have similar, although not identical, experiences. They don't usually share about things that are completely unconnected.

In your donor report, begin with a phrase like, "We wanted to know about...., so we went to ask the people who received our help about that. After talking with several people, including men, women, teens, and the elderly, this is what we learned." Then tell *their* story in brief terms.

This is where your statistical data comes in. After you describe the impact you want your donors to know about, show how widespread that sort of impact is based on the numbers that represent change. That makes it more factual and less anecdotal.

For example:

We spoke with 60 women who completed the literacy training program. Naturally, their experiences were different in some ways. However, 46 of them told us about three important things they all experienced.

First, they said literacy training was giving them economic power in their households because now they could be employed in higher-earning jobs. In the past, their husbands controlled the household money. Many of them wasted it in on drinking, gambling and prostitutes.

Secondly, the women shared about how they had gained a sense of self-worth. Previously, they were viewed more as property, with no sense of self-identity or worth. Now as literate income earners, they felt self-worth, which produced self-esteem.

Thirdly, they shared how their new sense of self-esteem was emboldening them to try new things and to continue their learning path. This gave them hope for a brighter future. They said it was something they could pass on to their children.

When asked what we could do better, they didn't hesitate to make several suggestions. We were all ears!

One organization started their donor report with this simple yet profound impact story. They added simple statistics to show it was not just a one-time event.

> *"It wasn't the quality of their education that impressed their neighbors. Those people didn't seem to think improved employment opportunities for the women was that unusual. What did impress them was that women in the program were obtaining a driver's license. In fact, 90% of the 423 women in our program did indeed earn a driver's license."*

Why was having a driver's license so impressive? It was because driving was evidence of true equality and freedom from male oppression. With opportunities, women could receive better education in this country. They could find ways to earn more income, yet driving a car was a symbolic threshold these women had crossed. To their female neighbors, this was success at the highest level for the organization that trained them.

These two examples contain some important elements which should impress donors.

- Their core education program is effective. Women were being educated. The ultimate goals are being achieved.

- Neighbors have taken noticed and are impressed, at least with the driver's licenses. This is third-party confirmation.

- There is statistical significance. This is not just an outcome for one or two people.

- In one case, it shows a positive unintended surprise. The Western-run training school didn't realize women's driver training was a key to cultural transformation.

Admit Failures

It's okay to talk about what didn't work so well. Transparency is important because most donors know that in the real world things don't always happen according to plan. One faith-based organization leader said sometimes he thinks he has raised more funds talking about what didn't work well than what did.

For example, providing written literature in a region where the majority of the population is non-literate was a mistake. The information they were trying to communicate never made much of an impact because it was generally inaccessible. The important thing is, the leaders were able to explain what they learned from that mistake, and what they did about it.

Rather than distributing print material, they shifted to distributing their materials on audio devices. Now people could listen and understand the important health, safety, and biblical lessons the organization was trying to communicate broadly, and then change began to happen. Ebola infections decreased by 75% among a population of 68,000 people. Fifty-one thousand people possibly avoided death. There were less contagious people unknowingly spreading the disease, and new Bible knowledge brought hope that improved other areas of their lives.

Turning failure into success demonstrates your organizations dedication to your cause. It makes you far more attractive to donors who who want to make a noticeable difference in their giving. So admit your mistakes. However, be ready to explain what you learned from it, and point to what changed as a result of that learning experience.

7.

Staying Up to Date

Much of what has been written in this book can work well for organizations that are not stagnant or on decline. Your organization may be generally new, and new organizations don't typically need to deal with legacy practices that hinder progress in a changed world.

Over the last 60 years, there has been quite a surge in the growth of nonprofit organizations. The Berkeley era, or if you are faith-based, the Jesus Movement, generated a lot of idealism, which birthed a lot of do-good organizations. And many of them have done a lot of good. If those organizations are still around, they are operating in a world quite different from the one that inspired them in the first place.

Applying the advice in this book may be more challenging for older organizations that have not kept up with change. Collecting good impact data assumes your structures and strategies can deliver the sort of impact regular and high capacity donors want to fund. Your business model can demonstrate effectiveness in generating good results. However, if you struggle with describing your business model, then this section provides some advice on how your organization can re-invent for relevancy—and donor dollars.

Four Ways to Keep Up with Change

These days many well-established social service agencies and faith-based nonprofits operate on a significant bet. The bet is the funds they raise will achieve good results. Mission is driven by practices built on time-honored tradition. Organizational legacy keeps them within tried-and-true boundaries and paradigms. Group think hinders their ability to keep learning. As time marches on, the odds are increasingly stacked against them.

Change is no respecter of legacy or tradition. Science keeps discovering, inventors keep inventing, innovators keep disrupting, and creative processes keep getting more creative. And, oh yeah, culture keeps changing. This thought seems trite. Everyone knows change happens, yet many do not look out for it, seek to understand it, adjust to it, or even acknowledge it. When this happens, an organization's effectiveness declines. Irrelevancy is not far behind. Over time, people—along with their funding—move to where they think they can achieve greater results. It's nothing new.

When mainline church mission funding became institutionalized, donors who had been historically more intimately involved in mission endeavors became simply a funding source for official church missions and ministry. This disenfranchisement caused them to reduce their giving, eventually shifting the bulk of their giving to the grassroots parachurch movement of the late 20th century. There they knew how their funds were being used. The money move disrupted traditional mission practice, and it's happening again.[54]

Are the older parachurch organizations responding to this shift? Not much. So now donors are disrupting things again by moving their money to a surprising new place. Rather than giving to middleman organizations, their charitable funds are increasingly going into a donor-advised fund (DAF), where, as one writer put it, money goes to wait for good ideas.[55]

A DAF is like a family foundation. Donors have full control of their giving with a charitable tax deduction. DAFs put them in more control of how their funds are used. In fact, about 48% of foundation grants ($24 billion in 2013) were given by these family foundations, and Gen X donors are among the biggest users of DAFs.[56]

Even so, the funds are still largely waiting for good ideas. This fact is based on the expenditure rate where more is going into the fund, but only a small amount is going out to causes. This presents a big challenge for nonprofit CEOs. According to a MissioNexus survey, it's their biggest challenge.[57] Agencies need to demonstrate that they are worthy of DAF investment, and that is a problem if their organization is still operating in older paradigms.

Disrupt Yourselves

As the old saying goes, if you keeping doing the same things, you keep getting the same results. However, because the world changes, you get diminishing results. For organizations to keep up with change they need to occasionally disrupt themselves before donors do it for them.

A speaker at the Innovation and Entrepreneurship for a Disruptive World Forum explained it this way: "Disruptive means, innovative ideas that disrupt the status quo when the status quo is no longer effective in achieving mission and impact."[58]

Disruption sounds negative. We usually consider disruption as something annoying because it interferes with processes. Managerial leaders are usually the ones most annoyed over disruption since their job is to ensure smooth operations. When creative staff promote new ideas, it is usually managers who react quickly with detailed questions. They tend to ask the "prove it now" questions.[59]

Yet innovative ideas take time to prove. New practices need space to learn and improve. Managers have important work to do, but they should not be leading change, according to change management guru

John Kotter.[60] Rather, lasting change can be more successfully implemented if top leadership is championing it, protecting it, modeling it, and resourcing it.

Four Steps to Self-Disruption

The following action items can help any social nonprofit or faith-based agency improve performance. Doing these things require patience, discipline, and determination simply because they are disrupters of the status quo.

1. Ensure New Learning (Bust Your Own Myths)

Over time closed groups, such as working teams and departments, develop group thinking. As a result, learning decreases, work culture becomes entrenched and resistant to change. Faith organizations (e.g., missions and churches) tend to draw on internal staff rather than hire an outside expert to help them think about what needs to change and how.

Nevertheless, it is important these leaders to bring in such corporate outsiders because, without external feedback, leaders don't know what they don't know. A good consultant can skillfully ask the "dumb" questions. Dumb questions are questions leaders assume answers to and never talk about. A good consultant knows how to facilitate discussions that examine basic assumptions which drive the organization.

So often, the leaders will discover they don't assume the same things, and what they do assume often no longer fits with the times. External consultants help with this important discovery process. In a way, they are disruptive outsiders who bring the team together to develop fresh insights. This is necessary because of organizational group-think, which stifles creativity and innovation.

2. Foster Group Diversity

The notion of crowdsourcing is not as much about numbers as it is about diversity. The more diverse knowledge, experience, and wisdom brought to a problem, the greater the chance solutions will be found. Even on a small scale, diversifying is disruptive when new staff join a team, especially if they are younger and seem a bit brash. So often, solutions arise when this kind of disruption happens. It can be discomforting to a team that has enjoyed their comfort zone for a long time. Nevertheless, if you want to achieve greater success with the resources you have, then make yourself and your team a bit uncomfortable by mixing in staff members who have different perspectives.

3. Maintain a Safe Climate

How safe do staff members feel when exercising creativity within the organization? Are they afraid to raise an issue, ask a dumb question, or suggest a crazy idea? Do they have space to try new things without fear? Typically, a hierarchical structure prevents creativity from flourishing. Reporting structures may simply make trying new things too daunting. Supervisors may fear losing authority or control.

Some order needs to be maintained to ensure good operations. However, if creative and innovative work is not flourishing on the margins, finding ways to move the tested results to the core, the organization will lose its effective edge. Leaders need to ensure that people have the freedom and safety to try new things and even to fail. That is, if failure is not overly expensive and produces valuable learning that moves the mission forward.

4. Budget for Change

Many nonprofit organizations have accepted conventional thinking that small overhead cost attracts more donors. If donors really are impressed with small overhead, then they may be betting on a losing proposition. Large, inefficient overhead is not helpful either, but budgeting for self-disruption is necessary. Designating funds for trying new things shows the organization wants to improve performance. If done well, the return on investment will be greater organizational effectiveness, more measurable results, and relevancy.

Donors should look for organizations that use their budget to ensure they are smart, informed, always learning, and thus well-situated to achieve good results. That is where donors will find the good ideas their DAF funds have been waiting for. If an organization hasn't budgeted for reinvention, they should search for a donor who understands how their funding in this area can make changes for greater good sooner.

The rate of change in the globalized age requires nimbleness, flexibility, intentionality, and perseverance. Rethinking strategies, operations, and mission values is not a luxury only if you have the time. Rather, the future of your organization may depend on it.

8.

So What, Church?

In the U.S. a church is by nature a nonprofit organization, so they are not obligated to register with the IRS as such. The term 'church' is found in IRS codes, however it is not defined. It is loosely described with a list of characteristics.[61]

Even so, many churches have registered as 501(c)3 nonprofit charities for a variety of reasons we won't go into here. Registered or not, all churches are accountable to the IRS for how they use donations much the same way secular nonprofits are. They just have less IRS reporting obligations.

Not paying taxes and not being controlled through mandatory registration was meant to keep churches free from government control or influence. But one thing is clear, at the time tax-free status was given, the Government believed the Church's role in helping the poor, the homeless, and providing general moral training was good for society.

According to one research report, if churches were taxed using a standard corporation tax rate of 39%, the IRS would collect $71 billion dollars per year.[62] That figure provides a hint about how much money passes through churches annually.

As with other kinds of nonprofit organizations, churches are still accountable for producing a lot of good for their members and for society. This notion of producing spiritual and social impact with untaxed dollars, and especially tax-deductible gifts from church members, is important.

Even if unregulated, accountability for use of church funds still stands. Moreover, in the faith sector there is greater accountability before God for creating more good with church funds.

What kind of impact are churches producing with the funds entrusted to them? Perhaps church income is declining because member trust is steadily eroding. The reason for this may be because members simply don't think the church can produce much impact with greater giving.

Tithers Asking the So-What Question

The elders of one church complained about a wealthy member who wasn't giving as much to the church as he was capable of giving. He was giving less than ten percent of his income, but his giving was still a significant amount compared to middle income givers. Why wasn't he giving more?

During previous times it might have been considered sacrilegious to question church elders on their use of member donations. Yet it was this lack of accountability that led to the loss of mainline church funding, with the bulk of giving going to the parachurch.[63]

Church member money is on the move again. This time it is going to non-church causes. Charitable giving has rebounded since the 2007 financial crisis, yet church income is still declining, as it has for the last ten years. One reason for the decline is church membership has slipped a bit, but there are other reasons.

8. SO WHAT, CHURCH?

There are far more faith-based nonprofit causes now than ever before. Their impact goals are usually clear. They understand consumer marketing, so fundraising campaigns use all the tools of the trade to attract donations. They don't tend to be open-ended, so donors know they aren't stuck for life in giving to their cause.

Even so, as the authors of *Passing the Plate* explain, the issue isn't just about competition for donor dollars. Instead, they say its these nonprofit causes' "basic narrative and worldview that captures people's imaginations and commitments."[64]

It's not like church members are withholding tithes from the church and giving it to these causes. It's because they would rather give to these causes than to the church.

It is common knowledge that most church giving comes from a small number of generous givers. Many of these people are the same high capacity givers who also donate to non-church causes. As already mentioned a few times, they are withholding more giving from charitable causes until they see a worthwhile project that will release more giving.

It's the same with giving to churches. The rich church member who the elders complained wasn't giving enough was withholding for a reason. He didn't think the church would produce much impact with larger gifts. He was giving just enough to help cover church operations cost.

One high net worth church member put it this way:

> "*Giving money to my local church has, unfortunately, been one of my least rewarding activities in my social ventures. While I'm happy to give some money to help cover operational costs, the projects that churches tend to champion and support are too often lacking substance.*
>
> *I see churches rally support for a friend of the pastor serving Jesus in a certain country or for our missionaries that came from the church body. This support is given regardless of the merits of their mission. "Love offerings" and "opportunity to partner" with the church's missionaries seem to be more about the church body feeling good than it is about producing lasting impact.*
>
> *I have seen some churches set amazing goals, such as creating non-faith based after school mentoring programs targeting kids in the gap of social services, or working to adopt all special needs kids in a communities' foster care system. Those are initiatives that have real substance and community impact. And sadly, they are very rare.*"[65]

This is the problem confronting many churches today. They don't offer a compelling narrative describing impact goals that capture the minds and hearts of their members. The members default to giving enough to keep the church afloat.

Church impact metrics, if they share them at all, are the same as many mission agencies. It just focuses on numbers; people saved, baptized, Sunday morning attendance, Sunday school attendance, home groups started, and satellite churches launched. They don't talk about how lives are changing other than an occasional testimony.

Now the generous givers are beginning to ask the question, "So what, Church?" What difference are you making in people's lives, in community life, and in solving serious social problems? How are you planning for impact? How are you monitoring and reporting the results of your mission as the local church in the community? Church leaders do not have answers.

Who Is Doing the Spiritual Work?

Someone might argue the work of the Church is of a spiritual nature. Their job is to teach the Gospel so people can live spiritually and emotionally healthier lives. The destitute find hope and the hurting are healed. People find God and the Spirit begins His work. These goals, they may argue, are intangibles that can't be measured. Some would say it is sinful to even consider the notion.

If these things describe the mission of the local church, then could the church hold itself accountable to their spiritual impact goals by providing indicators that such things are actually happening? It seems there would be many stories that, pieced together, show how successful a church is in carrying out its spiritual mission in the community. This has nothing to do with boasting or presuming to know what God is doing. It has everything to do with *validating* the effective use of financial and human resources entrusted to the church.

Churches should monitor and evaluate results of the day-to-day rhythms of church ministry. These kinds of reports to the congregation would validate leadership and ministerial ability to make a visible impact with member giving. It could even release more giving from the normal 3.9% tithers who make up over 90% of a typical church.

This still begs the question, is the official local church the only one in the business of producing spiritual and social impact? These days there are large numbers of Christian ministries that work to produce the same results outside of official church. They do counseling, evangelism, and medical missions. They do discipleship training. They are involved in homeless programs. They practice intercessory prayer. They help wounded veterans and assist widows and orphans. They support foreign missions.

While they don't provide these ministry services in connection with a church, they are providing them nonetheless. They are registered nonprofit religious and non-religious organizations, and they are attracting more Christian donor giving now than ever before. This is for the simple reason that their ministry is clearly stated, tangible, compelling and reportable.

Indeed, this book focuses on such organizations, helping them know how to provide better impact evaluation data for their donors. Why has the local church exempted themselves from accountability for impact? It may have to do with basic theology.

Only About Generosity?

Preface remarks in the book *A Revolution in Generosity* helps us understand how basic biblical theology has presented only half of the Gospel mandate to produce good results.[66]

The book preface writer complains how Christian resource raising has followed a secular transactional model which has not achieved results. But this is true even for secular marketing lately. Transactional fundraising models are declining. He mostly speaks of a biblical call to greater generosity, avoiding the unbiblical practice of transactional fundraising.

This is praiseworthy, for who can argue against the call for greater generosity knowing how generous God is to his people? Theological statements of this nature are hard to argue against. Still, the writer doesn't stop there. He also makes distinctions between biblical stewardship and philanthropy, with the latter being an "unbiblical" practice. He points out how, "Business world practices in giving are saturated with ideology...divorced from biblical principles."

Trying to persuade people to give more money without helping them develop a greater sense of personal satisfaction and ministry fulfillment in their giving is not a good model for church or secular causes. Treating church members like an ATM machine doesn't show spiritual love for the giver.

Still, based on church giving statistics, this long-standing theological appeal to greater generosity doesn't seem to have had any noticeable effect on church giving. Does it have to do with a lack of vision around impact? Are church members struggling over the tension of being faithful to their church and the desire to make a greater difference with their giving?

To make a *biblical* argument, achieving good results in giving is a pretty strong mandate. If people entrusted with God's money don't achieve good results in their giving, the Bible says their money will be taken away and given to someone else who will produce more good with it. (Mat. 25: 14-30). This sounds suspiciously business-like.

Simply stated, to raise more money these days, churches need to demonstrate this principle of achieving good results. Then people may trust them with more of their money. Don't be mistaken. This is not consumer-capitalism. It's just a simple concept. Do what you say you do and provide evidence that good things are happening, then people will be willing to give more.

Raise Funds for Impact Not Buildings

The church elders decided it was time to relocate the church. They were presented with the opportunity to purchase another church that was shutting its doors for good. The new church property had a better location with greater visibility. It was close to the newly-remodeled, hipster-oriented downtown, with more attractive restaurants, coffee shops, and pubs.

This youngish church needed to improve facilities at the new church property, so they provided a brochure to their members listing the needs with associated cost. They even held an initial fundraiser to build awareness and understanding, but it didn't generate many extra gifts.

The members were already concerned about relocation cost. Some questioned the need for the improvements, at least for now. The pastor and elders believed these improvements were critical to their mission, but they didn't explain it very well. Their selling points all evolved around material things, so all the members could think of was the cost of building improvements and equipment. It was all rather uninspiring. Therefore, the leaders did something mid-level church leaders rarely do. They sought the advice of a consultant.

The consultant recommended they try something else they'd never done before; raise funds for impact instead of buildings. The idea was rather simple. People generally understand why you need a building in basic terms, but they usually don't know about the sort of spiritual and social impact a building can produce.

Following the consultant's advice, the church leaders applied the reverse logic planning model described in Chapter 4. They began by forming a compelling vision for how they wanted to impact their members and the community. After spending the most time on that, they briefly listed the needed *inputs*, that is the facilities with associated cost needed to achieve the impact they had described.

Table 12 gives examples of leading with impact rather than buildings.

Table 12. Examples of Church Impact Goals

Impact Goal	Input Item Needed	Opportunity
Build new relationships with the downtown culture through a relevant, safe, and welcoming church venue	New Church Campus Look	$80,000
Increase capacity to serve more students and families with quality facilities	Classrooms	$150,000
Community children's health and education strengthened and enriched	Adjacent house and property for community services	$440,000
Improved quality = fulfilled happy kids. Build stronger community relationships. Also generate income.	Gym Improvements	$65,000
Safe, healthy, diverse forms of exercise makes happy kids, which makes happy parents.	New Playground	$32,000

Starting with the impact you desire to make on people and the community is more inspiring. It helps people envision something in their mind's eye other than a building. They understand what *they* can help to achieve in their church and community through their giving.

Measure Results Not Activities

Like many nonprofit organizations, churches like to talk about their activities. Witness twenty minutes of announcements on a Sunday morning surrounding church activities, such as youth groups, college groups, retreats, short-term mission fundraisers, etc. You know what your church does. Do you really know what they produce through all of these activities?

Willow Creek Church wanted to know what they produce so they developed an impact evaluation program called Reveal. They wanted to know what church culture, methods, activities, and discipleship programs actually produced in their members. They weren't excited about their findings.

The evaluation revealed they were good at getting people to come to church, but like many attractional church models, they were failing in helping people grow in their faith. As a result, spiritual growth and maturity remained weak.

Church members who increasingly live out their faith could generate a lot of impact stories from their homes, schools, workplaces, and community in general. What a church says it produces through their people could be measured by periodically gathering evidence for spiritual improvement and its benefits.

Imagine reporting these kinds of impact stories to the congregation. But if discipleship programs, as Willow Creek Church discovered, are not producing mature believers who live out their faith, then impact will be lagging. This is also important to know. As with the nonprofit sector, owning up to failure in a church's local mission could actually attract more member giving. That is if leaders are willing to propose new compelling plans that that capture their member's imagination and commitment.

The call for church impact metrics is nothing new. Leith Anderson, writing for Christianity Today in 1999, argued churches need to move beyond statistical impact as a measure of effectiveness and address the more intangible attitudes and perceptions that indicate success. It's good advice many churches have yet to follow.[67]

His examples were progressive at the time, but they fall short on describing what ultimate impact evaluation should be for churches. Attitude and perception improvements should lead to action. Action should produce observable examples of positive change. What are church members doing outside of the church building that is influencing positive change in other people and situations? What does

8. SO WHAT, CHURCH?

that change look like? How is it increasing? These are tangible real-life examples that can be described or told in a story.

The following are some examples of what could change because of spiritual life being played out in the community. It is all measurable and documentable.

- Civic organizations are engaged by believers to address social problems in the community.

- Church members are teaming up with their local Young Life leaders to serve disadvantaged kids.

- School budgets to meet the needs of poor students are supplemented by church member fundraising.

- Homeless families are receiving rehabilitation help to get back on their feet.

- Believers are volunteering to help young latch-key children.

- Pregnancy counseling is providing healthy alternatives.

- War-scarred refugees are receiving help to establish safe and healthy homes to restart their lives.

- Foster kids aged out of the social welfare system continue to receive help to adjust to life as adults.

Church programs and individual efforts bring the light of their faith to all of these scenarios. Change will happen and impact data in the form of stories will reveal it.

Raising Money Outside of Church

As the pastor explained it, the members of his large church were feeling donor fatigue. They had just finished a major capital campaign to provide more space for the growing church. This church had been active in the community for years, managing a food pantry for the poor and providing help for homeless families. But the poor were still among them and the homeless population only increased. They asked themselves the "what difference are we making in the community" question. They reached the conclusion that it wasn't enough.

Going back to church members to ask for more campaign money was unwise, considering their fatigue over fundraisers. Instead they decided to expand their partnership in the community. They began working with a faith-based homeless rehabilitation organization, one not associated with any church. Building a collaborative and trusting relationship took time.

They also responded to their city government Request for Proposal (RFP) for working with the homeless. If their proposal was chosen, they would receive 3 million dollars in grants to help solve the homeless problem in their community.

Responding to an RFP is a lot of work. Nobody is going to entrust you with that much grant money without seeing a clearly stated plan with accountability measures in place. You have to provide a clear description of how you are going to tackle the homeless problem. You need to demonstrate that you have the capacity to run the service programs to achieve desired results. Impact results with clear benchmarks must be clearly defined. Program impact evaluation methods finish off the proposal.

Were the church leaders acting unbiblically in pursuing a significant grant in partnership with business-minded city managers? On the other hand, why would anyone provide a large grant or gift to a church without knowing if they had a clear plan and was capable of achieving the city's desired goals? Oddly, this same question rarely comes up in many churches because it is associated with a secular business thinking. Perhaps this is why generous church givers—typically business people—are withholding generosity. They don't see their giving as a gift to the church. Rather they view it as a grant that is meant to achieve some clearly defined spiritual and social goals. To make a grant, so to speak, they would need more information; the kind of information the church worked so hard to provide in their proposal to the city leaders.

To increase major gifts from generous church members, churches need to provide enough information to alleviate concerns about waste and ineffective ministry.

Applying methods described in this book for planning, monitoring and reporting on tangible change in people's lives because of the spiritual work of the Church can release more member giving. The Bible instructs believers to be generous *and effective* with the use of money. Congregants hear a lot about the generous part. Church leaders need to help the generous givers give effectively.

9.

Final Word:
Live Safe Gets Another Chance

By now you understand that doing qualitative impact evaluation is important for non-profit organizations (including churches) who want to improve on their own bottom line, which is transformational change in the people they serve. That sort of change should generate a lot of evidence that confirms your methods are effective.

Anecdotal evidence in the medical research field has little credibility. It should be the same way with nonprofit faith and social sector services. One-off stories may or may not be indicative of results. Your donors need more. They need enough stories to see clear trends developing. They need to know your methods are going to produce lasting change over time. Problems are being solved. Old methods are being replaced with more effective ways of working.

Doing qualitative evaluation is important for understanding what is changing in people and how that change influences their lives and the life of their community. Adding numerical support—your beloved statistics—will show your stories are actually typical and not just one-time events.

Thankfully, you are not out to impress the pros with your theories and scientific methods, although you do need to do evaluation well enough to be credible with donors.

Now you can share the full story of success, failure, trials, creative thinking, and solutions. It's all part of your story. Share those stories of impact with potential new donors and see how it can release more giving.

Live Safe's Second Chance

Live Safe's fundraiser learned some hard lessons from his interaction with the funding proposal reviewer. After the meeting he and his organization had to reconsider practices that have driven their fundraising for so long.

In the past, anecdotes and photographs were indeed generally effective in raising funds. People assumed good things were happening. They believed organizations knew how to carry out their mission. They thought one-off stories demonstrated broad results.

Live Safe learned that times have changed. They also realized they didn't know how to reform their organization at the core to focus on long-term sustainable impact. Their leaders had been thinking the same way for so long. So they disrupted themselves.

They hired a consultant to evaluate their structures, methods, how they talked about themselves, and how they marketed their mission. The evaluation process was emotionally difficult at times. They had to rethink cherished practices; what should change, what should they keep doing?

With help from the skilled consultant, they also discussed how they would plan for lasting impact from the start, rather than thinking about that after wells were dug and water pipes laid. Next they decided on methods for monitoring and evaluating impact at each stage of the project.

Because of the unpredictable nature of water projects in poor isolated villages, they chose a developmental evaluation approach. This would allow them to monitor effects more closely and make changes more quickly to keep things on track.

They could do qualitative evaluation in the process, gathering stories on how planning, training, collaboration, and implementation were affecting the people they desired to help. They could track how children's health was improving and how improved health was improving other areas of their life.

This approach provided them with significant stories for reporting to partners and donors on a regular basis. Problems would expectedly arise, and these stories were essential for transparency. Transparency builds trust between partners.

Luckily, the Live Save fundraiser was given another chance to make a presentation, so two years later he returned to the foundation leader who had rejected his first funding proposal.

This time, instead of coming with reams of statistical data and anecdotes, he came with stories. But not just a collection of disconnected stories. His stories showed progress. The stories demonstrated how people's lives began to change and how those changes began to transform communities. The evidence was beyond anecdotal. It was reliable and compelling. Their statistical data showed results were widespread.

The foundation leader was impressed. They decided to make a larger grant than Live Safe was requesting. Live Safe had successfully helped a donor release more giving.

Addendum

Impact Planning Checklists

This section provides a planning checklists, summarizing challenges, warnings, methods, and processes in impact evaluation and donor reporting. Use these lists to develop topical discussions with your organization's impact planners, evaluators, and fundraisers.

1. Challenges

- ☐ Problem of response bias (usually in favor of the funder).
- ☐ Bandwagon bias: interviewing people in a room rather than individually.
- ☐ Cultural impediments to candid feedback.
- ☐ Avoid feeling the respondent is being tested and could fail the test.
- ☐ Reducing qualitative results to a number. Does that explain things?
- ☐ Avoid perception of exploitation or intellectual property theft when collecting stories.
- ☐ The development workers find it hard to explain impact to the donors.
- ☐ Project managers tend to measure what is easiest or what they know how to measure.
- ☐ Respondent assumption that we only want to hear good news.

- ☐ Things that all relate to impact, that need some sort of measurements, to know how one thing is affecting the other.

2. Methodology: Measurement Design Process

- ☐ Project stages: snap shots of early stage, mid stage, late stage, and post-project period.
- ☐ Probabilistic analysis—Collect short-term indicators of long-term effects.
- ☐ Iterative methods to improve value of information gained.
- ☐ Business case for project design. How will this deliver the impact we want?
- ☐ What do we already know well? What do we know least about our impact?
- ☐ Current state of uncertainty: What do we need to know?
- ☐ What area(s) do we need to measure (well-defined)?
- ☐ Keep it simple, avoid the pull to complexity.
- ☐ What information in those areas has the most value—what has less
    - Qualitative (For understanding change)
    - Quantitative (To know how much change there is)

3. Define What We Need to Measure to Avoid Measuring the Wrong Things

- ☐ First, separate out what you do know from what you don't know.
- ☐ Focus on what areas? Knowledge transfer, moral behavior, church participation, voluntary actions, relationships, leadership, culture change, job success?
- ☐ Need clear, precisely-defined impact that matters.

- [ ] Location specific areas of impact measurement. Evidence of transformation that is relevant to the people's situation: treatment of women, for example.
- [ ] Define what decisions depend on the measurement results (this eliminates measurements that have less value).
- [ ] Define difference between measuring for uncertainty and measuring for risk.
- [ ] Value of impact measurements for different project teams. How much are we willing to spend based on the value of the information for each team?
- [ ] Break down what we need to measure: what is easier and what is hardest.
- [ ] Give examples of impact we want or expect.
- [ ] Things that are detectable and observable.
- [ ] How much data do we need? Less than we think.
- [ ] Does cost of measurement exceed benefit?

4. Domain of Measurement[68]

- [ ] Causality—What causes problems, and suffering, hence how to deal with it.
- [ ] Broken relationships with people and God affects self and affects others around us.
- [ ] Other new relationships effect relationship with others (information brought to the community by the restored).
- [ ] Time: cyclic, enslaving, end-point, purpose on earth.
- [ ] Ritual: rituals that enslave, those that respect, and those that are freeing.
- [ ] Injustice: marginalization, treatment of women, children, lack of ability to overcome impoverishments.

5. Reporting Goals

- [ ] For donors, data may need multiple formats to speak to left-brain and right-brain people, i.e. emotional case and intellectual case.
- [ ] Seek to share our findings with those we serve (financial partners and org partners).
- [ ] Make the reporting data *useful* for all partners.
- [ ] A method that a non-statistician could understand.
- [ ] Whenever possible, math is converted into simple charts.

6. Measure Does Not Necessarily Mean Count

It more typically means to determine a range of impact with a good probability of being true.[69]

- [ ] Random samplings. Not randomized controlled test, per se.
- [ ] Population proportion sampling.
- [ ] Spot sampling: snap shots of people and processes at certain times.
- [ ] Clustered sampling: random sampling of groups, then conducting a consensus of a more concentrated sampling within the group.
- [ ] Stratified samples: different sample methods used for different groups. Compare results.
- [ ] Experimentation: Anything deliberately created for the purpose of observation (test group and control group).
- [ ] Bayesian: determine how much we know and how that knowledge is changed with measurement information. Start with your qualitative knowledge, gathering information, update your subjective knowledge with new information.
- [ ] Assess people who are not affected by the funding or the project in terms of employment, cultural leadership, church leadership, etc.

7. Dialogue Methods

☐ Keep questions precise and short.
☐ Avoid loaded terms.
☐ Avoid leading questions.
☐ Avoid compound questions.
☐ Help refresh memory.
☐ Establish common ground.
☐ Be patient with stories, at first.
☐ Expect metaphors in response to abstract questions.

Endnotes

Author, website references, and personal comments in order of occurrence.

Chapter 1. Introduction: Live Safe's Dangerous Assumption

[1] Wiktionary.org/wiki/so what

[2] Jason Saul. 2011. The End of Fundraising: Raise More Money by Selling Your Impact. San Francisco: Jossey-Bass, p. 29.

Chapter 2. Impact Isn't Just a Number

[3] Christopher J. H. Wright. 2011. Samuel, an Old Testament Model of Accountability and Integrity, in (Ed.) Jonathan J. Bonk. Accountability in Missions: Korean and Western Case Studies. Oregon, Eugene: Wipf & Stock, p. 21.

[4] Bruce Wydick. What Secular Academics Can Learn from the Faith-based Development Community. Across Two Words, August 19, 2015. http://www.acrosstwoworlds.net/?p=408

[5] Chimamanda Ngozi Adichie. The Danger of a Single Story. Https://www.ted.com/talks/chimamanda_adichie_the_danger_of_a_single_story

[6] Ken Stern. 2013. With Charity for All: Why Charities Are Failing and a Better Way to Give. New York: Double Day. Kindle edition, location 236.

[7] The 2007 Study of High Net Worth Philanthropy. Issues Driving Charitable Activities Among Affluent Households. Nov. 2010. Bank of

American and Merrill Lynch. The Center of Philanthropy at Indiana University.

[8] Ibid 2010 Study.

[9] Mario Morino. 2011. Leap of Reason. Managing to Outcomes in an Era of Scarcity. Washington DC: Venture Philanthropy Partners.

[10] Philanthropic Landscape. CCS. 3rd Edition, 2014

[11] Dan Pallotta, quoted by Eden Stiffman in, Philanthropy Urged to Invest $500 Million to Track Results. The Chronicle of Philanthropy, October 05, 2016.

[12] Jason Saul. 2011. The End of Fundraising: Raise More Money by Selling Your Impact. San Francisco: Jossey-Bass.

[13] Angie's List is a US-based website containing crowd-sourced reviews of local businesses meant to reduce the risk of hiring unknown service companies.

[14] Eden Stiffman. 1 in 3 Rich Donors Held Their Philanthropy Back. The Chronicle of Philanthropy, August 30, 2016.

[15] The Generosity Project. Latest Trends in Millennial Giving. ECFA Webinar, 8 Highlights from the Generosity Project Survey. April 20, 2017.

[16] Drew Lindsay. The Future of Philanthropy: Where Individual Giving is Going. The Chronicle of Philanthropy. October 05, 2015.

[17] Ibid, Drew Lindsay.

Chapter 3. Impact Stories = Your Narrative

[18] Ken Stern. 2013. With Charity for All: Why Charities Are Failing and a Better Way to Give. New York: Double Day. Kindle Edition, location 420.

[19] A forthcoming book entitled Towards an Understanding and Practice of Spiritual Metrics by David Bronkema, Mark Forshaw, and Ellen Strohm (Eds.) will cover the topic among Christian development Agencies, Mission organizations, schools, and churches.

[20] See Chapter 7 in Jane Wei-Skillern, James E. Austin, Harman Leonard and Howard Stevenson (Eds.). Entrepreneurship in the Social Sector. Sage Publications.

[21] http://www.pewinternet.org/2010/12/16/generations-2010/

[22] Pew foundation states born after1997, while others say in the1980's, or even after 1985.

[23] John Kania, Mark Kramer, and Patty Russell. Last Word on "Strategic Philanthropy for a Complex World." SSIR | 14 | Summer 2014.

[24] Douglas W. Hubbard. 2010. How to Measure Anything. Finding the Valuables of Intangibles in Business. Hoboken: John Wiley & Sons. Kindle edition, location 179.

[25] Thanks to William Bjoraker for his insights on how cultures change. International Journal of Frontier Missiology, 28:1 Spring 2011, p. 20.

[26] Drew Lindsay. What's the Big Idea? The Chronicle of Philanthropy. October 04, 2016.

Chapter 5. Planning for Qualitative Impact Evaluation

[27] Based on notes from Mario Morino. 2011. Leap of Reason. Managing to Outcomes in an Era of Scarcity. Washington DC: Venture Philanthropy Partners.

[28] Quote from Jason Saul. 2011. The End of Fundraising: Raise More Money by Selling Your Impact. San Francisco: Jossey-Bass, p. 231.

[29] Lucy Suchman and Brigitte Jordan. Validity and the Collaborative Construction of Meaning in Face-to-Face Surveys. In Judith Tanur, (Ed). 1994. Questions About Questions. Inquiries into the Cognitive Basis of Surveys, Russell Sage Foundation, pp. 241-256.

[30] Judith Tanur. 1991. Questions about Questions. Inquiries into the Cognitive Basis of Surveys, Russell Sage Foundation, p. 8.

[31] Ibid, Suchman and Jordan, p. 243.

[32] Norman K. Denzin and Yvonna S. Lincoln, (Eds.). 2013. Strategies for Qualitative Inquiry. Edition Four, Los Angeles: Sage Publications.

[33] http://opportunity.org/what-we-do/measuring-impact

[34] Ibid Judith Tanur. 1991, p. 18

[35] John Gerring. What is a Case Study, and What is it Good For? American Political Science Review, Volume 98, Issue 02, May 2004, pp. 341-354.

36 Robert E. Stake, 1995. The Art of Case Study Research. Los Angeles: Sage Publications.

37 Brent Flyvbjerg, 2013. Case Study. In Norman K. Denzin and Yvonna S. Lincoln (Eds.). Strategies for Qualitative Inquiry, Edition four, Los Angeles: Sage Publications, pp. 168-203.

38 Ibid. Robert E. Stake 1995.

39 Ibid, Flyvbjerg, 2013:182.

40 Cynthia F. Kurtz. 2014. Working with Stories in Your Community or Organization. Participatory Narrative Inquiry. Third Edition. Kurtz-Fernhout Publishing.

41 Based on Cynthia Kurtz's description of the process, p. 109.

42 Ibid, Kurtz, p. 339.

43 Rick Davies and Jess Dart. 2005. The 'Most Significant Change' (MSC) Technique. A Guide to Its Use. Care International. United Kingdom.

44 Next Generation Evaluation: Embracing Complexity, Connectivity, and Change. From a description of the Conference at Stanford University, November 14, 2013.

45 Michael Quinn Patton. 2011. Developmental Evaluation. Applying Complexity Concepts to Enhance Innovation and Use. New York: The Guilford Press, p. 23.

Chapter 6. On Marketing: How to Message Your Brilliance

46 Douglass Cobb. Issachar Initiative. Personal Conversation.

47 Gilles Gravelle. 2014. The Age of Global Giving. A practical guide for donors and funding recipients of our time. Pasadena: William Cary Library Publishers.

48 Michael Moody and Sharna Goldseker. Next Gen Donors and Their Plan for Greater Impact. Stanford Social Innovation Review. Feb. 12, 2013.

49 Robert Rose and Carla Johnson. 2015. Experiences: The 7th Era of Marketing. Cleveland: Content Marketing Institute.

50 Ken Stern. 2013. With Charity for All: Why Charities Are Failing and a Better Way to Give. New York: Double Day. Kindle Edition, location 420.

51 Eden Stiffman. 1 in 3 Rich Donors Held Their Philanthropy Back. Chronicle of Philanthropy, August 30, 2014.

52 Jason Saul. 2011. The End of Fundraising: Raise More Money by Selling Your Impact. San Francisco: Jossey-Bass.

53 Julie Dixon and Denise Keyes. The Permanent Disruption of Social Media. Stanford Social Innovation Review. Winter 2013.

Chapter 7. Staying Up to Date

54 Gilles Gravelle. 2014. The Age of Global Giving. A practical guide for donors and funding recipients of our time. Pasadena: William Cary Library Publishers.

55 Leon Nayfahk. Donor-advised Fund. Where Charity Goes to Wait. The Boston Globe, December 1, 2013.

56 Philanthropic Landscape. Executive Summary. June 2014, p. 3. HTTP://CCSfundraising.com.

57 MissioNexus CEO Survey 2013: Navigating Global Currents, p. 33. Https://missionexus.org.

58 Vijay Vaitheeswarn speaking at the Economist Conference: Innovation and Entrepreneurship for a Disruptive World. University of California, Berkeley, March 23-24, 2013.

59 Roger Martin. Two Words that Kill Innovation. Prove It. Harvard Business Review, December 9, 2014.

60 John Kotter. 2012. Leading Change. Massachusetts: Boston, Harvard Business Review Press, p. 147.

Chapter 8. So What, Church?

61 https://www.irs.gov/charities-nonprofits/churches-religious-organizations/churches-defined

62 http://www.newsweek.com/2013/10/25/are-churches-making-america-poor-243734.html

63 Gilles Gravelle. 2013. The Age of Global Giving. Pasadena: William Cary Library, p. 7,

64 Christian Smith and Michael O. Emerson. 2008. Passing the Plate. Why American Christians Don't Give Away More Money. Oxford University Press.

[65] Personal conversation.

[66] Wesley K. Willmet (Ed.). 2008. A Revolution in Generosity. Transforming Stewards to be Rich Toward God. Chicago: Moody Publishers.

[67] Leith Anderson. 7 Ways to Rate Your Church. Christianity Today, Pastors Blog. 1999. Winter.

[68] Material from Paul Heibert. 2008. Transformation. An Anthropological Understanding of How People Change.

Addendum: Impact Planning Checklist

[69] Douglas W. Hubbard. 2010. How to Measure Anything. Finding the Valuables of Intangibles in Business. Hoboken: John Wiley & Sons. Kindle Edition, location 179.